Courage in our Hearts™

~A Family's Love Story

Roz Stephen (signature)

Alex, Raz, Larry and

Charisma Stephen

Also by Alex and Raz Stephen

Discover Your Inner Treasure™ (Inspired by Courage in our Hearts™~A Family's Love Story)

www.NextLevelRiches.com (Training System)

www.MeetwithAlex.com (Transformation Coaching)

www.AlexStephen.com (Speaking/Coaching)

Inspirational Life Quotes...A Collection for your Daily Motivation

How to Care for Orchids: For Busy People

How to Have the Best Individual Education Plan (IEP) Goals: For Your Child's Education

Courage in our Hearts™

~A Family's Love Story

By Alex, Raz, Larry and Charisma Stephen

Life Transforming Treasures™
–Fulfill Your Life Purpose
www.LTT7.com

Family's Cause: "Stephen Family Education Fund." – To assist students in furthering their education.

Printed in the United States of America

ISBN-10: 0-9910797-0-1
ISBN-13: 978-0-9910797-0-4

DEDICATION

This book is dedicated to Raveena Jasleen Stephen, our beloved granddaughter, and to our future grandchildren and great grandchildren.

"Learn how one family triumphed in the face of seemingly insurmountable obstacles. You will feel their love for each other. You will be encouraged and inspired. You may cry. You may laugh. No matter how you react, you will find the courage to live your dreams and to believe again in the power of love to transform the experiences of individuals and families for generations."

Vincent Toran is a Life Coach and Motivational Speaker.

TABLE OF CONTENTS

ACKNOWLEDGEMENTS

Many thanks to the Divine for the gift of life and the courage to live it.

Vincent Toran, thank you for believing in our story from the first day, even before we started the book. You always insisted that our life story was a love – story that will impact millions of people across the world. An integral part of the process of getting this book together...from start to finish, you were able to extract the story from us with your insightful questions, edits and dedication. Thank you for encouraging us; indeed, you are a friend and mentor. We are grateful that you are on our team.

Claudia Moss, your energy, laughter and passion are contagious. When you interviewed me on your Internet radio show, the Claudia Moss LIVE Show, on www.Talkshoe.com, you described our story as an awe-inspiring, love story. As fate would have it, you became a major player on our team and encouraged us, also, while sharing your vision for our **New York Times** success. We appreciate your skillful editing. What a pleasure and a privilege to work with someone of your caliber and humility. Thank you, Claudia, for being our editor.

Dr. Jacqueline Lyew-Armstrong, thanks for your reviews, edits and feedback, as we wrote the initial drafts of our book. Thanks for sharing your perspective and experience as an adult facing hearing loss.

Eric and Cynthia Barber-Mingo, thank you for your friendship, for reading the various drafts of our book and for giving us constructive feedback.

Brian Ainscough, we appreciate you for the interview and the contributions you made to Larry's life as his soccer coach, friend and mentor.

Pastor George Saylor, you are greatly cherished for your friendship, review and feedback on the manuscript.

Dr. Julie Van-Putten, we thank you for your suggestions and viable input in helping us put the finishing touches to the book.

And last but never least, Les Brown, we are grateful to you for being our speaking coach, helpful mentor and humble friend. You have inspired us by blazing an immutable light on our path. A powerful presence, you are truly appreciated for helping us develop our story so that we can impact millions across the world.

~Alex, Raz, Larry and Charisma Stephen
August 9, 2013

FOREWORD

Courage in our Hearts™~A Family's Love Story is a story that shines with the qualities of hope and possibility. Without these cornerstones embedded in their hearts, Alex and Raz Stephen could not have embarked on a monumental quest. Together, in the face of challenging life experiences, they, individually and as a couple, chose to grow certain characteristics in their personalities that other people facing a similar situation might not have chosen.

They had a willingness to face the unknown, not knowing what the future would hold when they traveled to a different country, not knowing how they would survive once here, and not having any idea of how they would handle the cultural or financial transaction. If we are honest with ourselves and view our lives in retrospection, we will find that we have run from the unknown, focused on a chasm of what might happen, and tried to control the future by thinking, 'I am only going as far as I can see.' And when we live by that creed, we take tiny steps instead of giant steps.

This family didn't shrink when summoned to engage the world. They were explorers on an adventure, a family releasing the controls of the outcome. Instead, they opened to allowing an attitude of gratitude to be the mighty tide to carry them into their destiny. Together, Alex and Raz embraced the moment with a sense of wonder, of mystery, of joy to whatever the journey would bring, as long as they were together, embracing the mission of seeking a quality education for themselves and their Deaf child.

Along the way, each member of the family, from the parents to the children, Larry and Charisma, had to develop courage, a belief in themselves and the strength that they could accomplish whatever they set out to achieve, not allowing any person or thing to overshadow their goals.

Diversity is what makes the Stephen Family unique and strong. They live diversity in terms of their religion, in terms of their son marrying a young woman from Singapore, in terms of a non-speaking child and one who does speak, and in terms of a non-hearing child and a child who hears. The Stephens are very rich in the celebration of their faiths, individually and collectively. Most families cannot make this claim.

Theirs is more than a love story; it is a story of hope, commitment, resiliency and embracing diversity.

This book is a lifesaver, a life changer. An incredible love story, it paints an unforgettable portrait of what is possible when two people decide to create an awesome life for their child. It is a story of courage, faith and determination. A vibrant illustration of never giving up, **Courage in our Hearts™** is transformative. Open it, and take your life to the next level!

Les Brown is a world-renown Speaker, Author and Media Personality based in Orlando, FL.

"To understand love we need to understand its spiritual meaning, to measure it by what it can accomplish. I personally believe that love can heal, love can renew, love can make us safe, love can inspire us to be our best, and love can bring us closer to God."

~ Dr. Deepak Chopra ~

INTRODUCTION

This is a story of love and courage and an indefatigable will to walk the path of one's destiny. **Courage in our Hearts™~A Family's Love Story** narrates that story in an unforgettable voice. The story's narrative voice is resplendent. It is an amalgamation of voices coming together in a symphonious melody to paint the portrait of what happened over the course of the Stephen Family navigating the Unknown to experience abundant blessings in a new environment.

Theirs is a journey that is most often heralded in classic literature. Usually, it is the tale of a male venturing into the world, forsaking family and the familiar, to forge his way to a truth, be it spiritual, personal or financial. With **COURAGE**, it is the leaving-home theme played out beautifully, and even enhanced with the standing up as a family unit, which made for reinforced love and support from one another, as their family and friends were left behind in Trinidad. Not only did the family stand strong, they stood up, academically and otherwise, and made their mark individually and in unison, as whole, independent and loving souls.

If you are like me, you will be wholly mesmerized following two fearless young people in love through the trials of their shared walk. You will rise and fly with them when they decide that turning back is not an option. You will beam with joy when Larry and Charisma grow up and take their place as successful adults in a loving family unit, determined to succeed, despite shifting circumstances, sometimes hard and sometimes harder. And you will dance to know, in the final pages, that their journey doesn't stop. It is only beginning, same as yours. Their question: Are you ready to embrace your destiny, to live out your full potential?

Claudia Moss is an Author, Poet, Speaker and Talk Show Host from Waterbury, Connecticut.

Alex, Raz, Larry and Charisma Stephen

"Progress is impossible without change, and those who cannot change their minds cannot change anything."

~George Bernard Shaw~

LESSON 1

LOVE

"Love recognizes no barriers, it jumps hurdles, leaps fences, penetrates walls to arrive at its destination full of hope."

~Maya Angelou~

Alex, Raz, Larry and Charisma Stephen

Sweethearts, Raz and Alex visiting family and friends in 1977

ALEX

Falling in love is such a beautiful and blessed miracle. At the age of ten, I envisioned the type of woman with whom I wanted to fall in love and eventually marry; she would be intelligent, beautiful, possess a sense of humor and be a loving mother to our children. I did not know how she was going to look, but I knew how she was going to think.

Though I knew about Raz, I have no memory of her when we were growing up in Trinidad. We met when I transferred to Raz's high school for two years of advanced-level, university-preparation classes. Raz was brilliant and, at fifteen, was promoted one year above her classmates due to her high academic achievements. She had then and still has beautiful hair and a warm, radiant smile. We greeted each other when I entered the school. However, we didn't become friendly until eight months later. I recall the principal introducing the students in the advanced class and saying, "Make friends, but that does not mean you have to get married." Remembering his comment now, I realize one never knows where jokes may lead.

Raz had Zoology labs right before our Geography class, and by the time she reached our classroom, all the seats were taken.

"I'll save you a seat tomorrow," I joked. The next day she took me up on it.

Actually, I had been saving the seat next to me for another classmate, but I kindly asked him to find another seat so that I could keep my promise. He was confused but left quietly. Unbeknownst to him, his kindness laid the foundation for one of the greatest relationships of my life. Raz is my first and only girlfriend. There were a lot of girls at my new school, but Raz was and is special to this day! We both loved Geography and, interestingly enough, our son Larry's first degree is in Geography.

Our relationship began when we were eighteen and sixteen. We deeply loved and respected each other. Although we did not agree on everything, we discussed options and respected each other's opinion. There were times when we had to learn to compromise. We learned by trial and error and by staying true to our values. It was not always easy, but every trying moment was worth what we now have.

We dreamed of attaining a higher education, getting married, having beautiful children and a loving family of our own. Thus, each day we did everything together. We enjoyed talking as we walked to Raz's home after school. From there, I traveled home by taxi. We saved our allowance to purchase ice cream or go out to eat occasionally. I recall on a Zoology trip once, we stood in heavy rains talking and getting soaked while everyone ran for shelter. Eventually, after my first dinner at Raz's home, she told her mother, "This guy is someone to marry." And she was right!

We juggled school, extracurricular activities and our relationship, sometimes sacrificing seeing each other so that we could achieve our goals. In Raz's final year in school, we saw one another once a month for a year in order for Raz to concentrate on schoolwork. Later when I graduated from high school, I worked in Port-of-Spain, in northern Trinidad, leaving home at 5:00 A.M. and returning at 7:00 P.M. Needless to say, the experience left me exhausted.

Meanwhile, Raz worked in one of the southernmost towns. We talked maybe three times a week on our work telephones, as I did not have a telephone in my house. This was the only way to communicate with Raz when I could not see her in person. At that time, we did see each other on the weekends, though, but those were trying times for our relationship. Miraculously, despite being apart physically, we grew closer spiritually.

Our commitment to each other deepened, and our love manifested in different ways. When we started our first jobs after high school, we jointly took a loan for our first major purchase, a new 1977 Datsun 120Y. I still remember the registration: "PW 7331." We bought the car to facilitate our relationship. It

7

allowed us to see each other more frequently, enjoy trips to the island's beautiful scenery and beaches and visit relatives and friends. Five years later, wholly enamored with one another, we decided to marry and found ourselves faced with one of the toughest tests of our love. Since Raz is Muslim and I am Christian, we had to choose a religion for our wedding and, later, inevitably, another for raising our children.

RAZ

Alex and I walked into the kitchen where my parents were sitting at the table, silent, as if they were already talked out. The air in the room felt heavy, and I knew today would be the day. My eyes skirted to Alex, who gave me a reassuring glance, before we greeted my solemn parents.

My father, Farook, greeted us and gestured for us to sit across from him. Although his brows were tense, I reminded myself that I was twenty-one, his firstborn and stronger than I gave myself credit.

"Dad, I love Alex. We love one another," I began. "And the whole family loves Alex. He has been coming here to see me for five years. It is time, isn't it?"

My dad's face was set in a tight resolve. I hated seeing him so serious, so I said, "He has dinner here more times than he eats at his own house. Doesn't that count for something?"

Alex smiled and lowered his head, staring at his hands on the cleared table.

Farook was not amused. "I know you are of marrying age, Raz. And you know we love and accept Alex as one of the family. That is not the issue here."

My mother reached over and gently touched my dad's hand.

Shifting his attention from me to Alex, my dad said, "Do you realize what you and Raz are doing here?"

"Yes, sir. We talk about it almost daily now." Alex glanced at me, to see if I wanted to share what we had surmised.

I nodded, then looked at my beloved father and bit my bottom lip. "When we said that we were getting married, we looked into how to get married being that we practice different religions." I took a deep breath. "I know who I am, Dad. I am a Muslim, and a strong one." I paused, reaching out to stroke Alex on the shoulder. "And I know that Alex is a devout Presbyterian."

9

"We know that, sweetheart," my mother spoke up. "What your father and I want to know is who is going to convert faiths---you or Alex?"

"Mom, just yesterday when we talked about where to have the wedding, I originally thought we could get married in the Presbyterian church, without me having to convert to a Presbyterian."

When I paused for emphasis, my dad raised a dark brow but remained quiet.

"After a thorough investigation, we discovered that I had to convert to Presbyterian, if we were to marry in the Presbyterian church."

I could see my father's jaw setting. So I quickly added, "But if we marry in the Muslim faith, Alex will have to convert."

Simultaneously, my parents looked at Alex, as if I were finally heading towards the answer they wanted.

Alex smiled, squared his shoulders. "With all due respect, I am as strong a Christian as Raz is a Muslim, but I'm willing to keep the dialogue open for our best solution."

"And what would that be?" Farook asked.

"For one, Alex and I could take Mom with us to visit with the head of your mosque," I hurriedly offered, embracing my mother with my eyes. "Would you be willing to go, Mom?"

My parents engaged in a brief, unspoken dialogue, as they had been together for many years and loved each other dearly. Mom had even converted to Islam from the Roman Catholic faith for him before they married.

"Okay, dear. Your father and I agree. I will go with you."

Two nights later, Alex and I took my mother to see the head of my parents' mosque. We drove forty-five minutes away and spoke to the Muslim leader for over two hours in the mosque and for three hours at his house. Yet for all our talking, we left without a suitable resolution.

Farook was waiting when Alex and I sat down to dinner the following evening.

"Did the meeting lead to Alex's conversion?" He cut his brows at me, as if he were fed up with empty talk leading nowhere fast.

I straightened my back. "Dad, I am not going to change my religion, and I will never ask Alex to change his."

My dad seethed. Even though my mother rubbed his shoulder and patted his hands, he struggled to contain his rage. After a few moments, when he could speak again, he said, "If you get married in the Muslim faith, Raz, we will have a big wedding. Huge. I will stand the cost of the whole reception and all of the wedding; everything."

"No. We are not going to do that. We've decided that we are going to have a civil wedding. We did a bit more investigating, and the Presbyterian minister said that after our civil wedding, Alex and I could go there, and he would do a blessing."

I stared at my parents, my heart heavy but resolved. They were noticeably upset. My mom began crying soundlessly and continued for days afterward, nonstop. It was a difficult time for me. I loved my parents and didn't want to upset them, but later, when I looked back on that scene, I marveled at my strength. In that moment, I knew I had made the best decision for me and my relationship, and all was well in my heart.

In the end, there wasn't a religious conversion for anybody. Alex and I stood most of the cost for our wedding, but our relatives and friends helped us with money and other things. One of my dad's cousins made my beautiful wedding dress. Alex's aunt prepared an awesome wedding cake. We had a civil wedding, got blessed at the Presbyterian church, and enjoyed a lovely reception at Alex's parents' home, where laughter, music and revelry were the order of the day. Everybody, including my dad, attended. It was a joyful, memorable day!

Much later, when Larry was born, we decided on another religious matter. We didn't want our children confused, asking, "Are we Muslims or are we Presbyterians?" So I decided our babies would be christened Presbyterians, because their father was a strong Presbyterian. They would have a distinct foundation there.

As we worshiped over the years, we went to the Presbyterian church and to the mosque. Later, while we attended Howard University for two summers, the children traveled home by themselves. Throughout those summers, Larry and Charisma went to the mosque, because they lived with my parents.

ALEX

What has kept us together? Many things; but, most prominent, is that we discuss issues, consider input from others, respect each other's views, and come to a resolution with which we can both live. The key is that we do not let other people influence or change important decisions in our marriage. This is sacred to us. We value our friends and family, but we are independent and determined souls joined together with love as the foundation of our relationship.

Since a loving relationship allows you to identify and use your strengths, we discovered one of our strengths was to approach every situation as a team. In most instances, we handle our relationship as a business in terms of planning, discussing, implementing and tracking results, and anticipating challenges, reactions, resources, and exit strategies. The result is that we have a relationship where we have experienced more rewards than we could have imagined.

We have grown together on this beautiful journey, and we are just in our first forty years together. Smile. Raz is my one and only. I still feel the same joy I felt the Sunday I realized that I was in love with her. I was at home doing my chores, watering the vegetables in our garden. As I thought about Raz, a feeling of love washed over me. I was nearly overwhelmed. The memory is so fresh in my mind until it feels like yesterday. From that point on, there was no turning back for me.

RAZ

I was flattered and grateful that Alex saved the seat next to him for me in Geography class. With long, shoulder-length hair, he was very popular with all the girls in our classes, and he was the star of the school's soccer team. I'd previously ignored Alex, concentrating on my studies. We got to know each other during and after Geography class. In record time, our relationship intensified. We went out once and saw each other after that daily during school and after school. Our love was very intense from the beginning. We are inseparable and have been since high school.

My mother's side of the family is very large, has a great outlook on life and possesses the best sense of humor. Being one of the oldest grandchildren, I am very close to my aunts and uncles. Love opens doors, but some in-laws, in general, can attest to the fact that it can be difficult to get the combination to open the door in an extended family circle.

Alex's combination to the door was encrypted because my maternal family and his paternal family had unsuccessful, past relationship histories. I am in the third, consecutive generation of girls from my maternal family being attracted to two generations of boys from Alex's paternal family. The first-generation relationship ended in a tragic accident, the lovers being my grandmother's sister, Nilita, and Harold, Alex's uncle from his grandfather's first marriage. The next relationship ended in divorce, and the lovers were my mother's sister and another of Alex's uncles, this time from his grandfather's second marriage. Now Alex and I are the manifestation of both families' happily married pair, me being in the third generation of women from my maternal lineage, and Alex in the second generation of his paternal line. Considering our families' past, my grandparents, uncles, and aunts did not like or approve of our budding relationship, because they had no reason to believe our relationship would succeed.

Alex's grandfather had eighteen children from two marriages. Alex's dad was a child of the second marriage. Alex's uncle, Harold, was the firstborn, and about nineteen years old when he fell in love with my grandmother's sister, Nilita. Both were in love against their fathers' wishes. I do not know the exact details for the disapproval, which could have been for many reasons, including the fact that this was an interracial relationship, as Harold was of East Indian descent and Nilita was Black and Hispanic. One day, Harold, slipping away in the sweetness of a sultry afternoon, went to visit Nilita. On his way back from seeing his love, his heart elated yet heavy to leave her, he fell into a river. Later, having to keep the love of his life a secret and having been soaked to the heart in his fall, Harold developed pneumonia and died.

Through the years, family lore has it that Harold and Nilita's love became a whisper when Harold left, a whisper reminding everyone that love was all there is. It blew gently most times, more passionately at others, but always murmuring of a mighty love to come, a love that would fulfill their destiny. Most of the family paid no heed to the whisperings. Others wondered, and deep in my soul, after I met Alex, I knew the whispers were true.

On reflection, I now realize the first generation's love was able to survive because of the power of love itself. The second generation thrived in its appointed time and was a beautiful harbinger of the strength of the love to come. Thus, as a team, Alex and I were able to pass our first test of overcoming potentially negative family histories. Just like us, you can choose to work together, with love, for the duration. You can make your relationship what you chose to make it.

The close bond Alex and I shared dictated that we needed to do what was right for our relationship's future. Looking back at all we have accomplished as a team, we are very happy that we stayed united, and we were able to pass our second test of doing what was best for our marriage, family and children's future.

A couple of years after Alex and I fell in love, my uncles and aunts fully accepted Alex. In truth, they dropped the "in-law" and considered him their nephew. This happened because my relatives saw and experienced the love Alex and I had for each other.

We started our family foundation by taking what could have been destructive forces of different faiths, races, family histories, and at some times, a long-distance relationship and just boiled everything down to what was important to us. The constant became the union, all the rest was just noise. When your family foundation is strong, anything is possible. As a team, we learned to overcome many things including our third test, discovering Larry was Deaf.

As we reflected on the individual stories of our relationship, we started to understand the magnitude of our connection. As compelling as our love was then and is today, there was something bigger than both of us at play.

On the supernatural level, our union fulfilled the dreams of two prior generations. In each of those prior generations, there was a realization of the potential power of joining our respective families. Larry's birth solidified the victory. He was the first offspring of the combined families, his arrival uniting us forever.

Our parental love poured out when Larry was born. He joined the circle of love from our parents, family and for each other, as his parents. A few years later Charisma joined us, and that love extended even further; they were an extension of us.

Our love and commitment to each other was rewarded in ways that continue to astonish us. Perhaps our blessings were stored seeds, waiting for someone to persevere, so they could bloom through the obstacles. It is often said that "the third time is the charm." Our story is proof positive of the truth in that statement. Vincent Toran says, "We are each born into a story. It is the story of our parents, our families, our community, our country and, ultimately, humanity itself. How we live our lives is the next chapter in that story." We now understand the power and blessing of the shared story we were born into, and we are honored that we had the opportunity to carry our love forward to our children and grandchildren's generations.

Love possesses the transformative power to make us new. When I was ten years old, my paternal grandfather started living with us. He was verbally abusive to my mother. It was terrible and happened regularly while my father was at work. My mother is mild mannered and quiet. Conversely, I verbally stood up to my grandfather. Later in life, I realized that my spirit was broken, and I harbored anger from this experience, which lasted for a number of years. Actually, I did not realize how much this experience had eroded my self-image, until I was sixteen-years-old and fell in love with Alex and discovered myself. I was blessed when I realized our love had transformed and strengthened my spirit.

As I age, the core of my being remains ageless. Every morning when I look in the mirror, I see myself as sixteen, with the same smile and spirit. I feel happy and empowered like I can accomplish anything. When I cross the ages that end in zero, I am not discouraged in the least, because I plan to continue feeling my strong sixteen-year-old within, no matter what life brings me.

From the day that we committed to be together at that young age, we cannot imagine life without each other. We do everything together. We accept and work on our challenges, and we celebrate our victories. We thank God for His guidance, grace and mercy that He has bestowed on our relationship and our growing family. We are thankful in advance for the many blessings we will receive as the journey continues. It is not always smooth and a bed of roses, but a peaceful, loving and caring relationship does so much for your life, health, outlook and energy.

The power of unconditional love is magnificent. We really learned this when we received the blessing of our granddaughter, Raveena. We give unconditional love, and it is reflected back to us so brightly from her pure and untainted being. Love is the greatest key to living a fulfilling life. We were loved by our parents and family. That love developed in us as individuals, and now we are blessed to feel its powerful magnification.

REFLECTIONS

"Faith, Hope and Love--of all three, Love is the greatest."

1 Corinthians 13:13

1. *Love is powerful. Love is one of the greatest* and long-lasting forces in the universe. Love is the ultimate problem solver. Love heals and strengthens your love for yourself. Love can make you whole by piecing together the parts of your self-image that may be broken from past negative influences. You must allow yourself to receive it, and then you return it. When someone comes along and says he does not care about your past or your self-consciousness, because he is there to love you, let him. And he may say, "When I see you, I see magic."

2. *You need to wholeheartedly receive his love,* and let it give you the power and support to think, I am going to live my life for today from this day onwards. I am releasing the past. You can consciously decide to open the doors to set the darkness free and usher in new light. You can do it because you are worthy of his love. No mountain is high enough to obstruct where you want your love and life to go, once you have love and understanding.

3. *You must have love for yourself first.* *When* you move into a relationship and give unlimited and unconditional love, it will come back to you in unexpected ways. You will grow together. Love will emanate from you to your children and others around you. We have friends, neighbors, and cousins who tell us that we are their role models in terms of our relationship as a couple and as parents. We are humbled by that perspective, and we are grateful for the loving relationship that we have built. Love is one of the greatest miracles of life.

4. *"Success is a journey, not a destination."* *The* road will not always be easy. In life, love allows you to enjoy the good times and develop the strength to handle the challenges, which are sure to come. We grew closer through the fun times and the rough spots. We recognize that spending over forty years together is a great achievement. You can accomplish it, too. However, remember that it does not have to be perfect. Your experience may not fit the textbook sequence. However, you must be grateful, have your vision and make a commitment with faith and love.

5. *"It is better to have loved and lost, than never to have loved at all."* –Lord Alfred Tennyson. We invite you to open your hearts and

discover the miracle of love. Love is wishing for others what you wish for yourself: peace, happiness, perfect health, and abundance. It is never too late to start. There is no fixed time. The time is now! If you find love at eighteen or eighty, it is well worth it. Love has a boomerang effect. When you give and share it with others, it returns multiplied.

6. *There is no textbook way to live your life.* As long as you hold on to your dreams, make a commitment and use your stumbling blocks as stepping stones, you can create your own rewards. The timeline does not matter; you can deal with whatever life throws at you. Life presented us with our children at a young age, and now we are thankful to enjoy our grandchild while we are still young and in good health to relish our togetherness.

7. *Embrace and practice "The Circle of Love" in* your relationships.

"The Circle of Love"

- Love is the greatest gift you can give and receive.
- "The Circle of Love" starts with you loving yourself, and then you loving others, which is returned to you

multiplied, strengthening your love for yourself.

- Practice the golden rule: Do unto others as you will have them do unto you.
- The simple things mean the most.
- Show respect for the values of others.
- Forgive so that you will be forgiven.
- Work as a team.
- Sometimes you need to compromise for the good of the team.
- Agree to disagree.
- Celebrate victories, small and large.
- Practice open communication.
- Be courteous.
- Be mature and apologize.
- Be grateful for the kindness shown by your partner, children and life.

Alex, Raz, Larry and Charisma Stephen

LESSON 2

ACCEPTANCE

"Acceptance is not submission; it is
acknowledgement of the facts of a situation. Then
deciding what you're going to do about it."

~Kathleen Casey Theisen~

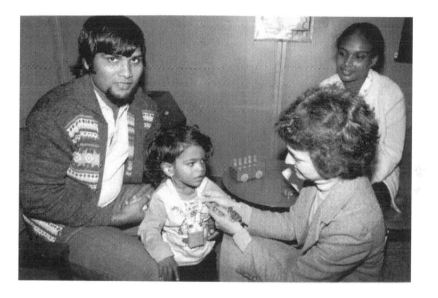

Larry received his first hearing aids in November 1980.

RAZ

On Sunday, September, 23, 1979, we had a big birthday celebration and christening for Larry's first birthday. It was the biggest celebration that we had since our wedding. Alex's family was there: his mom and dad, his dad's siblings, his brothers and sisters, and all of our friends. My mom and dad, my siblings, my mom's siblings and my maternal grandparents were there. On my side of the family, Larry was the first grandchild and the first nephew.

Our home was crowded. People spilled out onto the porch and into the yard. The warm Trinidadian air was alive with calypso music, and everyone was blissfully carefree. Our families were talking, laughing, joking, dancing and having a good time.

Larry was up. I had just fed him lunch and put him down for an afternoon nap. Alex and I opened the door to his room, which was close to the porch and off the living room. Near the end of the party, one of my aunts inquired, "Raz, did you notice that Larry slept through all the noise?" She stared at me in disbelief. "The baby slept through all the noise. He didn't get up at all?"

I looked over at Alex. We didn't want to believe her because she is the type of person who says things without thinking. When she said it, I figured she was just making a statement so I shirked it off, but she persisted, saying, "The reason why I said that is because my next door neighbor has a Deaf child, and I've noticed that before."

I was totally caught off guard. I had never suspected anything like that because Larry made baby noises and, sometimes, he looked back. I tried to erase it out of my mind, as Alex and I slowly walked into the bedroom. Alex clicked his fingers behind Larry's ears. Larry didn't look back. I lifted him, one mind reassuring me it wasn't real. He smiled, stretched from his long nap. My aunt's words weighed heavy in our hearts, and suddenly, things went from a joyous, festive mood with family and friends, to trying to figure out if our son was hearing or Deaf.

Alex knew a doctor in the hospital. He called him that Sunday night and told him about our concern. The doctor advised us to take Larry to the Ear, Nose, and Throat Clinic, where he worked. When we arrived at the clinic the next day, the doctor instructed me to sit in a chair and put Larry on my lap. Then he stood behind me and tapped a glass with a spoon. Larry didn't turn around.

"I'm sorry to say your son is Deaf," the doctor announced.

Alex, my mother, and I had tears in our eyes. I simply couldn't believe what was happening. "What do we do now?" I asked.

"Take him to the school for the Deaf," he replied.

We thanked him and walked out of the examining room. Larry was jolly and smiling as Alex carried him out of the clinic. He did not know what lay ahead, and neither did we. The adults were still in tears as we drove to the school for the Deaf. While we waited for the principal, Mrs. Donaldson, I peeked into one of the classrooms. What I saw shocked me! A teacher was beating the kids with a long plastic bat. She wanted them to listen to her, but apparently either she didn't know signs, or they didn't know enough signs. I cried harder.

Before long, it was our turn to see Mrs. Donaldson. Without hesitation, I asked, "What do we do now? When can he start school?"

She said, "Because of the large number of Deaf children, he will not be able to get into school for about six years."

In Trinidad, the large number of Deaf children was due to German measles. There was no vaccine in Trinidad, so babies developed the German measles regularly. I contracted it ten weeks into my pregnancy.

"He will be seven-years-old. That's too long. What can we do?" Alex probed.

The principal replied, "Well, I just came back from Washington D.C. from Gallaudet University. I spent two years there." She looked at us pensively. "You all are young. You should go to the United States at Gallaudet, and let your son have the best education possible."

Then just like that, everything happened fast, and seemingly all in one day. Without discussion or preamble, my heart decided that we would do it for Larry. I looked at Alex and our eyes met. We didn't say anything. We agreed without words.

It was a very sad day. The news had to penetrate us. We fell into a pit of 'What ifs' and looked for someone to blame. I asked Alex, as if he would know. "What if the immunization was available in Trinidad, and I had received it?" He didn't know how to respond to my grief. But I couldn't stop. "What if I got German measles at twelve weeks of pregnancy, instead of ten weeks? Then the German measles wouldn't have likely had any effect on Larry," I rationalized.

We spoke about it when we came home that night. "What are we going to do, Alex?"

"I don't know, Honey. I don't know, but everything is going to be alright," Alex assured me, talking himself into believing his words simultaneously.

I cried myself to sleep for several months afterwards, as I prayed, "Please let Larry be independent as an adult." Then in the midst of my teary sadness, I remembered the teacher at the school for the Deaf in Marabella. I recalled her beating the children with plastic bats as a way of communicating with them. Sadness overwhelmed me, and no matter how we struggled with the bleakness of Larry's condition, we floundered in the pit of feeling sorry for ourselves.

ALEX

A few days after we informed her Larry was Deaf, Ms. Arneaud, our elderly neighbor who lived next door, called me to her front porch. Standing in the morning brightness, she wore a light blue dress. Around us, the day vibrated with the music of insects.

"Alex," she called in her soft voice, "come. I want to speak with you."

I went across to the wire fence. "Yes, ma'am."

"I can see you and Raz. You all are sad. I can see your movements and how your spirit has dropped. Let me tell you something." She paused and looked into my eyes before she went on. "You both are young, and this, what happened here, could be the best thing that happened in your life."

The quiet conviction in her voice, in her words, raised the hair on my arms and legs. I didn't know what to say in response, so I said a polite, "Thank you." But in my mind I was thinking, What is this woman talking about? How could this be the best thing in our lives---to have a Deaf child in our 20's?

Now, when we look back at it in hindsight, Mrs. Donaldson and Ms. Arneaud were our angels, guiding us on our journey after we got such disconcerting news. By this time, Raz and I had already determined that we were going to do whatever was best for Larry's life. We could not wait six years for Larry to start his language development, education, and communication. We decided to take action to get Larry's hearing accurately assessed. We believed these actions were our lifeline out of the pit of despair. Over the years afterward, we learned to say to ourselves in difficult times: "When life gives you lemons, make lemonade!" This attitude instantly helps us spring into action.

Not long afterwards, we made arrangements to go to Mercy Hospital in Chicago to get an accurate hearing assessment for Larry and to discover if hearing aids would indeed help him. We made the trip in November, 1980. At the time, Raz was seven months pregnant with Charisma. Throughout that previous year, we hoped desperately that Larry's Deafness could be corrected, and that it would be the best possible outcome that would allow our life to continue as planned.

On our first trip to the United States, we found Chicago to be a foreign land; it was definitely a cold and windy city. This, added to what we were to learn, left us downhearted. By the most updated equipment, Larry was pronounced profoundly Deaf, with a bilateral, sensor-neural hearing loss. This meant his nerves, in both ears, were damaged, and hearing aids would not help much. Larry would not be able to hear or speak and would have to use sign language to communicate. He would have to attend a school for the Deaf. The worst possible news was our newly confirmed reality.

Our next stop was Gallaudet University in Washington, DC. While there, Larry underwent more tests, including psychological tests. It was determined that Larry was an intelligent Deaf toddler. The staff at Gallaudet said he was the perfect candidate for their program, and Larry was admitted to Kendall Elementary. We were extremely impressed with the expertise and facilities at Gallaudet, and our hopes brightened for Larry's future.

At this point, we believed we had fully accepted the reality of our life and were mentally prepared to immigrate to the United States. But although we'd made the commitment, still we harbored negative emotions of fear and anxiety. The solution was before us, but we were apprehensive. How were we going to make this tremendous change? Where were we supposed to start? How were we going to begin to immigrate as a family, with a newborn? Deep down, we were frightened of the uncertainties ahead.

We did the research and decided to immigrate as students. We needed to show over $60,000 in Trinidad dollars ($25,000 US dollars) to qualify for student visas, so we made plans to earn as much money as we could. We took out a loan to buy a taxicab, and, for two years, I drove the cab every day after my nine-to-five job and on weekends. Raz worked every overtime hour she could get at her job.

In the meanwhile, we stayed in contact with Gallaudet University, and they encouraged us to attend their summer learning vacation program for new parents of Deaf children. In June, 1982, sixteen months after our first trip, we attended the summer learning vacation.

When we arrived on campus, Larry was almost four. During our time there, we were able to interact with Deaf adults. Many were lawyers, doctors, and teachers, who were happily living normal lives. This was the first time we saw and spent time with Deaf adults. They were our angels, providing a 'light-bulb' moment. It was in that moment that we fully and totally accepted our situation. We knew exactly what Larry's future was going to be. We envisioned Larry being an educated, independent, successful, confident and happy adult, and we were compelled to commit to do whatever was necessary for Larry to attend Kendall Elementary School.

All the fear, all the anxiety, vanished. It was replaced with positive energy, and we had a crystal-clear vision for our mission. Our tears turned to courage as we embarked upon the journey which would allow us to create an extraordinary life for our family. We started moving in a straight line, the shortest distance, to our immediate goal of immigrating to the United States.

In September of 1982, Howard University accepted Raz. I took the SAT exams and received conditional acceptance at Howard as well. We acquired student visas, so we sold our personal car, the taxi, and the furniture. On Saturday, January 8, 1983, we went to the airport.

It is a cultural thing. In Trinidad, when one emigrates, family and friends come and see the person off. They bring food and drinks. It's an airport affair. Everybody was there, but we had mixed emotions; sad to leave, but hopeful that we were going to build a new future for ourselves and for Larry. We left Charisma with Raz's parents for six months, with my mom and sister helping out.

Simultaneously, we vacillated between sorrow and joy to see so many people come to see us off.

As we were heading to the Pan American flight, I held Larry in my arms, and one of my friends called me and said in a grave tone, "Alex, I want to tell you something before you go."

"What is it?" I replied, concerned.

"You will not make this with two kids, you and your wife in school full time, no jobs in a foreign country, no extended family and winter." The look in his dark eyes clouded over with worry. "You know what? I will pick you up next Saturday right here in this airport. You're never going to make it."

I was in shock, already feeling sad and leaving everything behind, trying to fight fear and think positive, and this is what this guy told me. I just looked at him. I didn't know what to say, so I said, "Thank you." I smiled. Little did he know that his statement would fan the flames of commitment in my heart. He'd done me a favor.

When things got tough and we contemplated returning home, I remembered my friend's words. I refused to go home without our education and Larry's level playing field.

We boarded a plane headed to Washington, DC, leaving our daughter and everything we knew in Trinidad.

REFLECTIONS

"You will see it when you believe it."
~Dr. Wayne Dyer~

1. *Whenever life gets complicated,* acceptance is a critical step to accurately assess the situation and determine how to proceed. Acceptance is a process, and at times it can be difficult to do. For many of us, where we are and what we are facing is the exact opposite of what we would like in our lives. But it is impossible to create a plan for moving forward if you are not willing to accept where you are. You must acknowledge all facts. When you release the resistance and the angst and allow things to be, you open up the space for options, avenues and blessings to occur. Life is a series of challenges and opportunities. Each of us will experience unexpected setbacks. We will be faced with fear and anxiety. We may find ourselves in mental, emotional or physical pain.

However, the first step in moving forward is learning to accept what is with faith, love and gratitude. This lays the foundation for creating the life that you desire for yourself and your family.

2. *The goal is to move beyond your* obstacles and challenges. Once you have a vision of where you want to be and make the commitment to take action, the right people, ideas and opportunities will come to you. Get a vision or partial vision of where you want to be. You must make a conscious decision. Do you want to remain stuck where you are and be there forever or will you decide this is not where you are going to stay? Your commitment to move forward will make you feel freer, happier, and you will actually start looking forward to your new journey.

3. *When you have full acceptance,* coupled with a vision of where you want to be, doors open, paths are created, and unbelievable solutions appear. You must be willing to believe in the power of your dreams made manifest! This is how it happened for us.

4. *Make the pledge to turn your* challenge into your opportunity to live your life's purpose. You can say, "I am in charge at some level, and faith is my co-pilot." This will help you get to the light-bulb moment of your future and give you the courage to proceed forward to a truly fulfilling and rewarding experience.

5. *Acknowledge your current reality.* Accept the challenges. You cannot change the past, but you can consciously choose to stop letting it influence your present life. Say, "I commit to being my best in the present moment, which is what determines my future."

6. *Failure to accept reality never* changes it. Drowning in sorrow does not create a path forward. In fact, sometimes, it makes things worse. Rather than tapping into the courage to move forward, you falsely believe that you are stuck. Yes, it can be difficult, but we believe that it is the only viable option. Release the negative emotions of denial, anxiety and fear. Let in the sunshine of faith and hope. We found that partial

acceptance results in slower progress. Total acceptance results in accelerated progress. Total acceptance is the bridge to your rewarding future.

7. *When we decided to immigrate to the* United States, we knew in our hearts we had to do this for our son. We did not think we were courageous, but we leapt with faith and just did it. We believed it was our only option. When we saw Deaf adults living our dream for Larry at the summer learning vacation, we knew we must take action.

8. *What can you do to get total* acceptance? Start your research. Talk to people who have overcome similar challenges. Join support groups. Tie your goals to what is important to you, for example, your children. Make a commitment to be a survivor. Envision your triumphant future. The clearer your vision of where you want to be, the more compelled you will be to get there.

9. *If you are facing a serious health* challenge, what is your vision for a perfect solution? Accept the current

facts, and make your perfect solution your mission. For example, a close friend of ours was diagnosed with prostate cancer at fifty. The doctors recommended surgery, but he decided he was too young. He started his own research and declared that he would beat the disease. He envisioned himself leading a healthy, cancer-free life. He radically changed his lifestyle by becoming vegan, eating only natural, cancer-fighting foods and exercising. Today, he is cancer free, brings his own food to parties, and is married to a woman who shares his beliefs and lifestyle. He has never been happier or healthier! Similarly, you have the ability to determine the course of your future.

10. *When you have a passion and a desire*, nothing stands in your way. Fearful, you may want to continue doing the things that make you feel safe and comfortable, but you need to listen to your heart and do what you believe must be done. This will give you the courage to accept the facts and move forward to attain your goals. Your ability to move forward isn't only for you. If you

have children, they are *automatically* learning how to deal with challenges as they observe you. When we say "automatically," we mean that no extra effort is required on your part. The information will be recorded as a statement about how to deal with life.

Alex, Raz, Larry and Charisma Stephen

LESSON 3

FAMILY

"There is no doubt that it is around the family and the home that all the greatest virtues, the most dominating virtues of human society, are created, strengthened and maintained."

~Winston Churchill~

Alex, Raz, Larry and Charisma Stephen

Larry and Charisma off to Trinidad in the summer of
1985

Courage in our Hearts™~A Family's Love Story

CHARISMA

I grew up in a very close-knit family. My friends and people I meet always tell me that they can see that we have a strong bond. I am very close with both my immediate and extended families. I was born in Trinidad, and at the age of two and a half years, I moved with my parents and older brother to the United States to pursue the "American Dream" of education and a better quality of life. Our life together has been a blessing to me in many ways.

It is common in West Indian culture for parents to leave their children behind to be raised by grandparents or other relatives, until they become established in their new destination, same as my parents left me in the care of my maternal grandparents for six months. I have met many people who have grown up this way, and, as a result, they have strained relationships with their parents. Sometimes these people move away from their island, and they long to be back with their grandparents and the people with whom they grew up. Even though they have more opportunities in their new location, they do not have roots there.

My experience is very different. My immediate family and I are close, in part, because of our move to the United States. We had no other family members here and, as such, we were all we had. My parents wanted my brother and me to grow up together. They did everything they could for us. And as we grew older, we truly appreciated them. I know how hard my parents worked while they attended college; I saw it firsthand. When we had a day off from school, they took us to campus with them. We met their teachers and friends. Consequently, we saw how everyone loved and admired them for their hard work.

After we moved to Massachusetts, occasionally, my dad would be reminded of jobs he held when he was in college. Often I could not remember the details, so I asked him, "When did you have that job?" My dad just chuckled and said, "Your mom and I had a number of jobs while we were going to school to support the family." All I remembered was that my parents created a loving environment for us.

My dad would narrate stories of the various jobs he held from the parking garage attendant to the Howard University banquet waiter. At times, he recalled Larry and me going grocery shopping with him and Mom. When we pulled up to the cashier to check out, Larry and I would have deftly dropped candy and other snacks into the shopping cart. My dad had to put the items aside because money was strictly budgeted in those days, and he said Larry and I would cry, breaking his heart. As small children, we didn't understand part-time jobs and the need to survive as students with a family.

When I was twelve years old and in sixth grade, my social studies teacher, Mr. Santos, asked everyone in the class to identify their role model. As he went around the class, many kids identified famous people such as Michael Jordan. When Mr. Santos got to me, I answered proudly, "I have two role models."

He said, "Two! Who are your two role models?"

"My mother and father," I answered. "They are my role models because my older brother is Deaf, and in Trinidad, if you are Deaf, you are dumb. My parents learned about Gallaudet University, the best school for the Deaf, which is located in Washington, D.C. They made the decision as young parents to leave our home in Trinidad and come to the United States in pursuit of a better life for our family.

"They went to school full time, worked part time and took care of us. They received high grades to maintain their full-tuition scholarships for the last three years of their undergraduate studies. As children, my brother and I saw firsthand the sacrifices they made to give us a better life. We look up to them and appreciate the hard work and sacrifice they made for us." When I finished speaking, a hush fell on the class, and I could see that Mr. Santos was very impressed.

I am the product of two cultures composed of many different people. Because my parents made sure that we visited Trinidad often, I am close to my

51

extended family there. As children, my brother and I spent two summers in Trinidad, while my parents remained in the United States, working. Those summers were the greatest. We grew up learning about our Trinidadian culture firsthand. We spent time every day with our grandparents, aunts and uncles. I think of my cousins as brothers and sisters because of that precious time we spent together. I love being close to my family. When we go home to Trinidad now, I still shower my family with love and affection. They mean the world to me. Trinidad is our second home.

I was raised to be always thankful for the blessings that my faith has given me. A gratitude prayer meeting is an important tradition to teach a child from a young age. It is a very important part of Trinidadian culture to celebrate blessings by having a prayer meeting and inviting family and friends to give thanks together for the blessings in your life. My maternal grandfather held these prayer meetings regularly: for having his daughter and her family home to visit from the United States and to celebrate birthdays, weddings, and graduations. For us, it was a family reunion. We would all get together to give thanks and have a delicious meal. Prayer meetings teach children gratitude, love, humility and how to focus on what you have, instead of on what is missing.

My extended family in Trinidad has always shown us love and acceptance. They do not look at my brother as someone who is different. He is simply another family member. A true testament to that is a number of family members learned sign language so that they could better communicate with Larry.

When Larry and I enjoyed Trinidadian summers, we lived with our maternal grandmother. Every day around lunch time she put my little cousin down for a nap. Afterwards, we sat on the front porch rocking chair and spent at least thirty minutes a day signing. We practiced the alphabet and basic signs. I loved teaching my grandmother sign language. It was great quality time for us. She wanted to learn how to communicate with Larry directly, without having to depend on me. She was able to ask him basic questions, such as, "Are you hungry? What would you like to eat? Do you want to go out to play soccer?"

My uncle Jamal is six years older than Larry. Larry and Jamal were very close when we lived in Trinidad. Uncle Jamal was our first relative to learn sign language. To this day, he still knows and uses sign language. Raaid is my uncle's son, my first cousin on my mom's side. He is three years younger than Larry. When we spent summers in Trinidad, we frequently went to my uncle's home. On my mother's side of the family, we have three female cousins and Raaid is the only male. Raaid and Larry played a lot and grew very close, and this closeness led Raaid to learn sign language, also.

And as a result, Larry and Raaid have remained close over the years.

Reyaz is my paternal aunt's son, who is seven months younger than Larry. He and Larry were close growing up, but I always had to interpret for them. Reyaz really wanted to do something special for Larry, so he learned to sign from a book and was excited to surprise us when we returned to the island. We were impressed that Reyaz took the time to learn sign language on his own. He, too, still knows sign language and is still close to Larry.

Growing up in my family and surviving the struggles, as well as seeing the results, have made me a strong, independent woman. My parents taught my brother and me about the importance of education by their example. We saw them get their degrees. We saw them become professionals with the ability to improve our quality of life. Larry and I learned that we had to work hard to get what we wanted. Opportunities would not be handed to us, but if we worked hard, sacrificed and poured our hearts into all things, opportunities would come to us and lead us to a better life. When I was seven, my mother told me that I needed to go to college and get a degree. She explained that this would allow me to work and have my own money. She instilled in me the importance of being independent and standing on my own.

I am the only person in my family whose life was not profoundly changed with the news of Larry's Deafness. To me, Deaf culture is a part of my culture. Since Larry is older than I am, I have been exposed to Deafness from day one. I could sign before I could talk and have always been around my brother and his friends. I did not have to learn about his Deafness later in life, I just grew up with it.

I love having a Deaf brother. His Deafness brought us closer. I was his interpreter in the hearing world. I was happy to be his ears and voice. In our family we shared unconditional love. My parents said, "This is your brother, you love him and you do what is needed to support him." They showed this by their actions, also.

Learning sign language as my first language created a strong bond between my brother and me. My parents learned sign language and strengthened their already strong relationship with Larry. The experience was new for them because they were raised in a hearing culture. But for me, it was all I knew.

According to my parents, when I was 2½ years old, as a family, we went every Saturday (for a few hours) to Gallaudet University, for years, to learn sign language. My parents attended the formal classes, while Larry and I played in the gym with the Deaf and hearing children of the other people attending classes. Usually Gallaudet students supervised the children. So being with Deaf children, Deaf adults and being a 2½-year-old child, I learned ASL and Deaf culture quicker than my parents. I was fully accepted in Deaf culture and the community, along with my parents, who wanted Larry to be a viable part of the Deaf community.

Some siblings make up their own language to communicate with each other while growing up. For us, we did not have to; we had sign language. It was like our family's secret language, and we could talk to each other around other people, without them knowing what we were saying. This came in handy when my parents wanted to scold us in public.

When Larry and I were little, we shared a bedroom. At bedtime, our mother would come in and say, "Ok, no more signing. Time for bed." To continue talking, we came up with the idea of signing in each other's hands. We thought we were geniuses. Later, we learned that people who are Deaf and blind, sign in each other's hands as a common practice. As kids, we thought we had invented something new.

When I was growing up, my inner circle of friends knew my brother was Deaf, and this was normal for me. My friends understood I was proud of my brother and not embarrassed by his Deafness. Occasionally I would encounter people outside my inner circle, and they would make ignorant comments about Deaf people or Deafness.

Sometimes their comments offended and hurt me. I would tell them that they should be more mindful of what they said, until I learned not to dwell on their crass comments, and to dismiss these people and their actions as unimportant.

It is hard for me to understand how some families with Deaf children do not learn sign language. In the summer of 2001, our family traveled to Rome, Italy, to support my brother at the Deaf Olympics. He participated as a member of the USA Deaf Men's National Soccer Team. When we were there, the athletes stayed in one hotel and the families stayed in another. I was so amazed to see how many families did not know how to sign. I cannot imagine my life without being able to communicate with my brother. To me, it is selfish to force your Deaf family member to write everything rather than learn how to sign.

I am proud of Larry's participation in the Deaf Olympics. He is passionate about soccer and has put in a great deal of hard work. He plays soccer with the heart, mind and soul of a soccer player. I used to interpret for him at soccer practices and at games. Larry's soccer activities were a huge part of our family life. Larry's being on the USA Deaf Men's National Soccer Team was an accomplishment that showed the power of persistence. No matter how many people told him that he could not play because he was Deaf, he never gave up and, consequently, accomplished one of his lifelong dreams!

Growing up, I thought all hearing families with a Deaf family member had to take sign language classes. When we moved to Massachusetts, my parents and I took sign language classes at The Learning Center for the Deaf (TLC) in Framingham, Massachusetts, where Larry went to school. The classes were a fun way to get to know people. I had an advantage because I had spent so much time with Larry.

Though Larry was older, I felt I had to look out for him because I could hear. If we were home alone, I could hear the doorbell, the phone, and the smoke alarm. During the winter in our apartment in Massachusetts, the fire alarm went off often at night when it was too cold. Whenever the alarm sounded, it was my job to wake Larry. Then I would knock on the wall to let my parents know that we were up. In the beginning, I questioned my parents about the necessity for me to do these things. My parents took the time to give me a detailed explanation of why my help was necessary. I appreciated their explanation especially since most of my actions were for our safety.

As Larry's baby sister, I was always with him, like a shadow. I was his interpreter everywhere we went, the playground, soccer games, etc. This made us close. When I was little, sometimes I wished I was

Deaf so I could go to school with him. In all of the schools he attended, the staff was nice. I also felt very comfortable with Deaf children. Thus, I always felt that I was as much a part of Deaf culture as Larry was. Interestingly, when we were around other Deaf children and adults, everyone thought I was Deaf. They were surprised to learn that I was a hearing child. They were amazed to see how close Larry and I were and how I interacted with his friends. They were also amazed at my ability to sign. I explained that sign language was my first language, and therefore, it was natural for me to sign well.

When I was five or six years old, on a car trip, I was looking at my brother's ears and asked my mother, "Mom, why did God give Larry ears if he was going to make him Deaf?" My mom giggled at me and thought my comment cute. At the time, I did not know that his Deafness was caused by my mother's illness with German measles (Rubella) during her pregnancy.

Then when I was 12 years old and about to enter middle school, I was vaccinated to protect me from German measles. I remember my mom looking at me with tears in her eyes. "What's wrong, Mommy?" I looked at her, wondering how she, too, could feel the shot.

She replied, "If I had gotten that shot when I was younger, our whole lives would be different. Larry would not have been born Deaf, and we would not have moved to the United States."

I have always been very proud of Larry; I call him "my baby." He hated it and often asked, "How can I be your baby when I'm your older brother?" But I felt this way because I had always charged myself with looking out for him when we were growing up. Even though I was younger, my additional responsibilities made me feel like the older sister in some ways. Larry was dependent on me to be his ears when we were alone and to be his interpreter to the hearing world. Today, it gives me a sense of pride to see him accomplish his dreams. His graduation from high school as valedictorian of his class was particularly special for me. Larry had worked so hard with his school work. When we were children, I remember being ahead of him in Mathematics, English and Reading. He viewed my progress as encouragement and soon surpassed me in his schoolwork.

When my maternal grandfather passed away, my brother, having been close to him, wanted to be a part of the service. Larry wrote a speech about the loving memories he had with our grandfather and how he was going to continue to support our grandmother. Our grandfather was very well known in his town. He was a teacher and a principal and very active at his mosque and in the community. At his funeral, there were over 600 people in attendance. When my brother stood up to tell his story, he signed, and my father interpreted. When they were reseated, I saw various expressions on many faces in the audience. For many, it was the first time they had seen a Deaf person like Larry. They were amazed at his intelligence and ability to tell his story about his relationship with our grandfather. I was so proud of my brother for being able to do that.

My brother has accomplished many things. He has graduated high school, holds an undergraduate degree and a master's degree. He is very active in the Deaf community and has started many organizations for the Deaf. He is a loving husband and doting parent, who always feels the need to give back and show others how he has been blessed.

When we go to Trinidad today, Larry enjoys visiting schools for the Deaf and talking to the students. Most of these students do not go on to high school; instead, they perform menial jobs, and if they are lucky, they learn a trade and work in that trade for the rest of their lives. They are raised believing that is all they can do, because they are Deaf. My brother shows them another option. He tells them that he was born in Trinidad, and he was able to go to school, finish high school and go on to earn two degrees. Now, he is a professor, teaching others. He offers them support and resources, and tells them they can be anything they want to be. My brother is an inspiration to the people around him.

"It's all about the power of unconditional love; it is great to be able to give and receive it."

~Charisma Stephen~

REFLECTIONS

1. *Upon reflection, I have begun to understand* how my brother's Deafness shaped our family; I believe it was God's will. In a sense, because of it, we have grown separately and as a unit. My parents have learned how to overcome any obstacle that stands in their way. They did not listen to people who told them that they would not make it in the United States, with two small children. They did what faith put in their hearts to do. They did it for our family, but it was not just for Larry and me. Our story has opened the eyes of many people. My parents did not take this news as bad news. They learned about the best options for their son. One of those options was a school in Washington D.C. They did everything they could to save money to give Larry a fair chance in life. Taking that risk and leap of faith taught our family and friends in Trinidad and in the United States about acceptance and persistence.

2. *Now our family has expanded. Larry married* Amrit, a wonderful woman, who is also Deaf.

We are very close and think of each other as sisters. They have a beautiful daughter, Raveena, who is hearing. With the addition of my niece, I can see firsthand what it is like to be a hearing child born into Deaf culture, and I feel as if I am getting a glimpse of my childhood. I feel very lucky to be a witness to that. Raveena and I are close and are very much alike. We both love music and love to sing and dance. Also, she started attending Montessori school at the same age that I did. We share a special bond, which I love and feel is our blessing.

3. *When I was little, I remember seeing my* mom's cousin once in Trinidad. Years later, when I was about twenty, I spoke with her on the phone. Her mother was sick at the time, and my mom called to check on her. When I greeted her, my mom's cousin said, "Charisma, you probably do not remember me, because I have not seen you since you were a child. Do you still give people a big hug as soon as you see them?"

Smiling, I said, "Yes, I always do that."

"Do not ever lose that quality, no matter how old you get." Her comment surprised me. I did not realize the impact I had made on my family and friends, because of the love I showed them. To me, it is just a part of who I am and me wanting them to know I care.

A few years later, I realized the full effect of my mom's cousin's advice. We were visiting my paternal grandmother in the hospital, and my dad's aunt arrived with her young granddaughter. While the other adults talked, I played with my little cousin. Days later, my grandmother passed. It was very emotional for me because we were close. At her funeral, I saw my little cousin. As soon as she saw me, she ran to me with open arms and hugged me. I knelt down and squeezed her. In that moment, I realized the significance of my mom's cousin's comment. It's all about the power of unconditional love. It is great to be able to give and receive it.

4. *Recently, my family and I went to a T. Harv Eker seminar together.* Everyone I met was so amazed that we were doing this as a family. To me, it just made sense. We started this journey together, why not continue it together. If we are going to continue growing and continue being success-minded, we must do so as a family, not only as individuals. What good is a blessing if you cannot share it with those you love? I love learning new things and sharing the experience with my family and friends. If something is giving me joy, success and happiness, of course, I want the

people I care about to have the opportunity to have the same experience!

5. *Family Jewels exist in every family. Take a* quiet moment to mine the jewels in your family.

FAMILY JEWELS

- Great role models exist in your immediate and extended family. Identify and utilize these role models.

- Appreciate and utilize extended family support.

- Thankfulness teaches gratitude, love, humility and appreciation for what you have, instead of what's missing.

- Enjoy the power of unconditional love.

- In a family, love can be spelled in various ways: acceptance, communication and appreciation.

LESSON 4

MISSION

"In achieving your goals, you may run into roadblocks. Don't let that stop you, go around, over, or under. If you are committed to your goal, you will find a way."

~Catherine Pulsifier~

Alex, Raz, Larry and Charisma Stephen

Alex receiving the Beta Gamma Sigma Academic
Achievement Award in 1985

ALEX

I remember it like it was yesterday.

Summer vacation was quickly approaching, and I begged my dad to buy new clothes and shoes for me. I knew there would be plenty of parties to attend, and I wanted to look good. I told him that I was sixteen, that it was more important than ever that I look my best. Surprisingly, he agreed.

My dad was the sole breadwinner in our home. I was one of his five children. He told me that I would have so many new clothes and shoes that I wouldn't need anything for the following school year. I was in heaven, imagining how great I would look at the parties and during the upcoming school year. Shortly thereafter, on a warm Sunday afternoon, Dad informed me that I would be joining him at work on Monday morning and that I should bring a change of clothes. He worked at Texaco Oilfield. This invitation was unusual because the only times I had been to the company before was to celebrate a promotion or a retirement. In part, I enjoyed those visits because there was always plenty of food.

The next morning, it seemed as though my mother and father were laughing at me, so I asked, "Dad, why am I going with you at 6:00 A.M.?" I couldn't imagine the role I'd play for this particular visit.

"To get your summer clothes," Dad responded in a joking manner.

On the way to my dad's workplace, I learned that he, a foreman at the company, had secured a job for me with one of their contractors. He dropped me off at my new work station, promising he'd see me at 4:00 P.M. With my breakfast and lunch in my lunch pail and a change of clothes on one arm, I introduced myself to my new co-workers.

I wasn't in their presence for an hour before it occurred to me the men were unhappy with their jobs and did not want to be there. With a supervisor and other employees, I climbed into a boat of some sort, and it was then the supervisor advised me to remove my clothes to my underwear and climb onto a raft in the middle of a lake of black oil. On the raft, my job was to join the men using a set of ropes to direct the excess surface oil in the lake into a recycling system. Apparently, this was a task that needed to be completed before breakfast. At its completion, I was drenched in the smelly oil. When I eventually cleaned the oil from my body with kerosene, I discovered the experience had caused me to lose my appetite entirely.

That afternoon Mom met Dad and me as we walked up the driveway towards the house. Dad was joking with Mom and laughing about how I had made enough money to purchase my first set of clothes.

Mom looked at my altered skin tone and didn't see the humor. "You will kill the boy," she said, scolding my father.

"Oh, sweetheart, he won't die, I assure you. He is my son, too, you know!" Dad laughed and embraced my apprehensive mother. "And if he does, he will be the first to die in that lake."

Mom was not amused and put her foot down. "That's it! Our son is not going back into that situation, and that is it!"

She stopped walking to drive her point home, and I knew I'd better speak right then, letting them know what I'd just decided.

Resolved, I looked at Dad and then turned to Mom and said, "I am going back! I need some new clothes!"

Dad laughed harder than ever at both of us.

Though I spent the entire summer working at the company in order to earn enough money for new clothes and shoes, it didn't take me long to decide that it was not the career for me. I was not spending the rest of my life there. Initially, many of the men were bothered by my presence, because they were there to support their families, and here I was a sixteen-year-old kid only looking to buy new clothes. What they didn't know was I went into the situation with life goals. In the long run, I was there for a short while to one day attend a university, get a good job, marry a great woman, buy a house, and travel the world. My goals did not sit well with them at first, but eventually I became great friends with many of them.

The entire experience started out as a great joke, but it motivated me to excel, as I refused to return to Texaco Oilfield after graduation. It was not a part of my goals and vision.

Some individuals are blessed with an early knowledge of what they want to do with their lives as adults. On occasion, we have crossed paths with those who have their entire life mapped out. However, many people realize what their true aspirations are after several years in school and in numerous unsatisfactory jobs.

Whether your mission in life becomes apparent at five or fifty-five is unimportant. What is important is that you realize it and begin to take steps forward.

"Burn the bridge of fear, and build the highway to success."

~Raz Stephen~

When you have your own powerful, driving goal and a commitment, it becomes easy to take action. Here are some guiding steps to put you on a mission to accomplish your goals. Moving through these steps leads to the creation of your "Abundance Plan."

Your WHY

Your WHY is the inspiring vision and compelling reason for you to achieve your goals. It needs to be strong enough to move you to action. It motivates you to persist and focus when you face challenges and obstacles. You must want to satisfy your WHY as much as you want to inhale the air you breathe.

Whatever your WHY is, write it down. You should define it clearly. You can even accompany it with pictures and music to bring it to life on your vision board. And most importantly, tie an emotional bow around it by relating it to what is important to you, for example, your children. Finding your WHY can help you gain confidence and manage risks as you work to achieve your goals. Identify your WHY now; it can be the difference between success and failure.

Use the following questions to help you identify your WHY:

- What is my vision?
- What do I want for my family?
- What drives me to achieve my goals?
- What legacy will I leave?

This is our WHY:

During our life's journey, the Divine has graced us to experience countless miracles. We are living our passion of sharing the lessons and wisdom we have acquired to empower and transform people's lives around the world. We want to help others overcome their challenges and create their own rewards for themselves and their families. We have established the Stephen Family Scholarship Fund to assist and support children who want to further their education and cannot afford to do so. Our future generations will carry on this legacy of helping others to transform their lives. It is important to us to spend quality time as a family, especially with our grandchildren. This gives us the motivation to excel, as we serve others.

Your Passion

Passion is being who you are and doing what comes naturally to you. To identify your Passion, ask yourself these questions:

- What do I love to do?
- What gets me motivated?
- What energizes me?
- What would I enjoy doing without getting paid?
- What will I do with my life once I retire?
- What is my favorite hobby?

When you are pursuing your WHY by using your Passion, ideas will flow. You can think outside the box. You may even get rid of the box entirely so that your creativity flows freely. You will be able to create services and solutions to help others. You will be so energized that your life will become more fulfilling every single day. It is important to believe that the world needs your contributions.

Your How

"If I have the belief that I can do it, I shall surely acquire the capacity to do it even if I may not have it at the beginning."

~Gandhi~

Goal setting is a powerful tool that can motivate you into making your WHY a reality. As you set and achieve your goals, you will build your self-confidence.

75

You can start by listing your goals, using empowering language in the present tense, instead of the future tense, with specific dates, times and measurable items. For example, "I have the outline for my book for review at the end of the month now." Precision is the key. Knowing exactly what you aim to achieve helps you to recognize it when it is accomplished, because you accomplish it first in your mind. Begin by brainstorming to come up with a list of possible options to pursue. Then review the list to determine what matters most. Once you have prioritized your list, create a new document. This will help to build positive energy. Set small tasks towards the realization of your goals. This will allow you to have early wins and will enable you to assess your progress. It's true. The journey of a thousand miles begins with one step.

"To achieve happiness, we should make certain that we are never without an important goal."

~Earl Nightingale~

You can set your goals in different categories:

- Personal
- Career/Business
- Giving back
- Spiritual

As you set your goals, think about leaving a mark or a legacy. Do not worry about how you will achieve it. The How will come.

It is our passion to share the lessons we learned to help you accelerate on your path towards your goals. Once you have identified your WHY, your Passion, and made a detailed list of your goals and the results you desire, the next step is to list your beliefs and values. To get the best results, you need to be as detailed and honest as possible when you make this list. We like to call our WHY, our passion, and our list of goals and beliefs, "Steps to Abundance." Whenever we use it, we inevitably create abundance.

Beliefs and values drive commitment and action, the effects of which are results. If your beliefs and values are aligned with your results, you will be compelled to make the commitment and take the actions to achieve your goals. If these things are not in alignment, you will have internal conflict, and you will not be able to make a wholehearted commitment to achieving your goals.

For example, if you believe you do not deserve happiness, great health, a fulfilling relationship or financial independence, you will not be able to attain those results. There will be a conflict with your beliefs and the results you say you want, and that conflict will restrict the positive actions you need to take to achieve your desired results. To help identify and change limiting beliefs, we recommend you read Dr. Joseph Murphy's "The Power of Your Subconscious Mind."

When your beliefs and values are 100% aligned and congruent with your results, you will be filled with excitement and energy. Ideas will flow. You will be motivated to work late at night and jump out of bed in the morning. In short, you will be living your life's purpose, easily sensing that the world needs and welcomes your individual gifts.

We encourage you to create an "Abundance Plan" as soon as possible. When you do this, you will discover insights about the beliefs and values that are preventing you from living the life you desire. You will be able to resolve the internal conflicts and begin to modify your beliefs and values, to get the results you desire.

To appreciate the power of creating an "Abundance Plan," think about something that you have already achieved which seemed impossible when you began. Make a list of the beliefs and values which propelled you forward. Are these the same beliefs and values you need to achieve your new goals? If not, what's missing?

Your Action

Our beliefs and values of faith, education, love for family, and setting high personal goals compelled us to take Actions that allowed us to get the desired results. When your beliefs and values are aligned, it is easy to go for it, because   each of us wants to live passionately engaged in life.

When we learned Larry was Deaf, we knew his future options were limited in Trinidad. In contrast, when we visited Gallaudet University in the United States, we saw Deaf adults who were lawyers, doctors, and teachers. They had their own families and homes and appeared to be happy and successful. This blew our minds! We began to believe that the opportunities for Larry were limitless.

Like Martin Luther King, Jr., we had gone "to the mountaintop and seen the Promised Land." We had a powerful, compelling vision of our son being an independent Deaf adult. We had a dream and a goal. We stopped being sad and worried about Larry's future; instead, we resolved to give Larry the best education possible, and this propelled us into action. We planned, worked and persevered to achieve our goal.

"Most people fail, not because they aim too high, but because they aim too low and hit. And some people do not aim at all."

~Les Brown~

REFLECTIONS

1. *There is no magic in small dreams.* The magic is in dreaming big and believing in your ability to achieve your goals. Never fear failing. Failure is only feedback about what does not work.

   We had one big goal, which was for our entire family to succeed academically in the United States. In our minds, achieving this goal was important to our family's survival. We wanted the best education available for our Deaf child, so that he could have the opportunities to live a normal, independent and successful life. We wanted to succeed academically at the university to get great jobs. We were focused on taking the steps necessary to achieve this big goal.

2. *It is common for parents to want their children* to be independent. What do you see as the path for your children to have a good life? We wanted both our children to have a bright future. We wanted them to be happy and successful. And in our minds, education was the path that would pave the way for them.

3. *When we immigrated to the United States with* our two young children, *we* were only high-school educated. Our parents' and grandparents' frequent mantra was:

80

"Education stays with you. No one can take it away." Thus, we wanted our children to be college educated. We made it a practice to visit universities. We started with universities in our home state, Harvard and MIT. On a trip to Montreal, we visited McGill University. We visited Duke University in North Carolina, Berkeley in California, and the University of Miami in South Florida.

4. *Encourage your children to appreciate school,* to excel and take challenging classes. Nurture habits like reading and a love for books. Nurture a love for learning and discovery.

5. *A driving value for us is always putting forth* our best efforts. General George S. Patton said, "If a man does his best, what else is there?" Indeed, what else is there? We encourage you to set high expectations. Set high expectations for yourself and your children. Teach your children by example. Encourage them to put forth their best efforts in everything they do, including schoolwork, sports, friendships and hobbies.

6. *Share your expectations and vision of your* children's lives with them. Start early, and if you haven't done so already, remember, it's never too late. Your high expectations will encourage your children to do their best. In

turn, they will become successful adults with great habits instilled in them for their own families and careers.

7. *Reflect on your dreams, wishes, and goals for* your family. Think big. Think great. You and your children can attain those goals. Turn your reflections into results, and use your beliefs and values to help you make the commitment to take positive actions. Focus on who you are and what you want for yourself. The purpose of the "Abundance Plan" is to produce rewards for you, your family and your future generations.

"Education is the key to unlock the golden door of freedom."

~George Washington Carver~

Alex, Raz, Larry and Charisma Stephen

LESSON 5

COMMUNICATION

"Even though we may be occupying one space, we are not able to communicate with each other."

~Larry Stephen~

Raz and Alex in Atlantis, Nassau Bahamas in 1998

RAZ

The moment I saw Alex I knew he had something on his mind. Solemn, so different from his usual jovial self, he smiled before we embraced in the middle of the living room. We were both exhausted from a long work day and, for a blissful moment, we simply enjoyed the sound of the other's heartbeat before we spoke. Alex was the first to break the silence, whispering his hello into my hair.

"Today it happened, Raz. Finally. I've dreamed about this day for so long." His eyes radiated a sudden gleam, his voice vibrating with a surreal excitement.

I grinned. "You never told me you were due another raise, Honey! Did the bank offer you another promotion?"

What else could it be? I asked myself. We were both working, and things were going well for us. We were meeting our expenses and saving for the future.

"It's even better than that, Honey." Alex took in a deep breath, held my hand and guided me to the living room sofa. He looked into my eyes intently, excitedly. "I have always dreamed of having my own business and being an entrepreneur, and now I can finally see where it's manifesting. I saw the separation package as a good opportunity. "

I furrowed my brows, tilting my head in curiosity. He was leaving too much unsaid. "One moment, please, dear, but what's going on at the bank, and why are you talking like you'll be leaving soon?"

"The consolidation at the bank happened and the new bank came in. Raz, this is my chance to leave Corporate America, something I've always wanted, remember?"

"But, Alex, we've talk----"

He softly stroked the black braid on my back, calming my opposition instantly. "I know, Honey, but I got the opportunity to get a very lucrative package if I leave now. I understand your concerns. Really I do. I've heard you. But this is the Universe lining up for me. This package with all of its benefits lasts over a year. It's perfect for my transition into my own business."

"What business are you speaking of? Real estate?"

He grinned, his eyes moving from mine to somewhere across the living room. "That was a while ago. I don't dream of it anymore."

"Alex, why must you leave now? We've always said you can do your own business when we retire.

We've spent so much money for the children's education, not to mention we have loans because of the children's education, and this is the opportunity now for the next 10 years to work and have the money to pay off those loans and build a nest egg and then when we retire in 10, 12 years, there will be a lot of opportunities to venture into your own business."

I inhaled deeply, my thoughts racing. How were we to live if he left the bank now? I pondered.

"Everything will work out. I know it. I want to be an entrepreneur; this is going to be the best thing for our family. We could make more money than being in Corporate America. We will have financial freedom. We will live the life of our dreams."

I sighed. "What about staying on for 3 to 6 months after this consolidation?"

Alex shook his head. "No, that won't work."

"Why?" I asked. "With the package, you either take it now or decline it and then look for a job within the bank?"

I folded my arms against my body, trying to understand.

Alex nodded. "Yeah, and the jobs are those where they put you, a square peg, in a round hole. That is what I've been seeing so far in the bank. People are going to jobs that they weren't trained for, so what happened was that after three months, six months, you get laid off and you don't get the package. So the best decision for me is to take the package and pursue my goal."

"Well, are you sure you want to do this? And I still don't think it's a good idea, but the package does look good."

"Raz, that is all I think about, being free of Corporate to work for myself. Yes, Honey, I want to do it. All I need is a chance. The package opens the door to my business goals."

I replied, "I just don't agree, but I will stand with you." I tried, but I couldn't help thinking that he would try this plan and maybe even try different other things and see that it's not working out and then eventually he'd go looking for a job again.

Alex said, "This is going to work out. This is my lifelong dream."

I didn't know how I wasn't supposed to be concerned. The change Alex wanted to make affected our entire family, and it was important for us to create the space for meaningful communication. We went back and forth for a few weeks after that. I held on to the fear of the unknown; we had loans, mortgages, and for him to just leave his corporate job was outside my comfort zone. But Alex answered my questions and addressed my fears. In the end, I was not going to stop him from taking the package.

Looking back, I cannot believe that I had concerns and fears. Once I gave Alex my full support, we were able to work as a team to achieve our individual and combined goals. Our communication created a space for greatness to happen. We were able to take the other's perspective and create a synergy to improve our ideas and create new ones, and to generate excitement, energy and renewal of efforts, so both of us could advance as a team.

REFLECTIONS

1. *I believe that within the context of a family, in* particular, we have to be able to say, "I love you so much that I want to listen and understand, but I recognize there are things that cannot be fully explained or understood. I hand you the baton of trust which says that I trust you enough to believe in you and your dreams." I could not pretend that I understood. But in my heart, spirit and soul, I knew that it mattered to him. And he mattered to me. So, I was willing to travel that road with him. Reaching a point of

agreement was a testament of our love for each other.

2. *We often forget that the whole purpose of communication is for spirits to commune.* To commune in this sense means to converse together with sympathy and confidence, to interchange sentiments or feelings, and to take counsel. In all relationships, there is a higher order than the individuals involved. In our family, we were concerned about our individual perspectives, but we were also sensitive to the impact of our decisions on the entire unit. We have learned that when we strive to commune our spirits toward one goal, there is no obstacle the family cannot surmount.

3. *Where there is resistance, things slow down,* and when there is no resistance, abundance is manifested. When we communicate with an unselfish love that says, "I wish for you, what I wish for myself; therefore, I am on board," it helps to resolve conflict and eliminate resistance. Now, as a couple and a family, there is unity to open doors for each member to flourish and to increase the family's abundance.

4. *Non-resistant communication is very rewarding and makes life easier. A great*

example of a relationship based on non-resistant communication is a close, sibling relationship. After you have out grown the childhood disputes, you experience a bond that can be effortless, and it is gratifying to have your sibling cheering for you. The relationship is based on love and support; there is no jealousy or hurtful criticism, only unconditional love and acceptance. When we decided to have Charisma soon after Larry was born, our intention was to give them the gift of a close, sibling relationship.

"Communication is the thread that knits families and relationships together."

~Alex Stephen~

5. *Though our experiences have had happy* endings, we recognize that not all interactions end this way. What do you do as a young adult who wants to pursue a direction that is significantly different than your parents' expectations? What if your partner refuses to hear or understand your perspective? These are very real situations and can be challenging to address. The first thing to remember is that the purpose of communication is for individuals to share their

experiences and perspectives. There is no guarantee that in the sharing you will build consensus. Once you realize that consensus is not forthcoming, you must make a decision. You can wait patiently for something to shift which allows for a resolution, abandon your plans or pursue them knowing that the other person does not agree with your direction. There are no easy answers. Effective communication is a process and, even in the best of situations, it requires knowledge of self, patience and understanding.

6. *Communication involves listening with love* and respect. Each person must listen not only to the words that the other person is saying but also to the emotions, which are the feelings behind the words. Recognize that the words are a substitute for the feelings the other person is trying to convey. This enhances the potential for understanding the messages that are being shared. It is important to respect the other person's point of view and wishes. Respect here means that you care enough to be truly engaged to make every attempt to fully understand the other. You are listening and paying attention with your ears, your eyes, your heart, and your spirit. This allows you to hear the unspoken. Often, the unspoken reveals hidden fears and positive motivation for the proposed action.

Think about how you communicate, especially within your family. Look for areas where you can improve your communication with your spouse, children, parents, siblings and friends. Obstacles and challenges should not deter you from communicating with your loved ones; they should have the opposite effect, which is to create opportunities for more communication.

LESSON 6

PASSION

"Adversity causes some men to break; others to break records."

~William Arthur Ward~

Larry representing USA Deaf Men Olympic Soccer
Team in Rome, Italy in 2001

ALEX

In Trinidad, the two major sports are cricket and soccer. I was passionate about soccer. My dad took me to see the professional games often. My youngest uncle, Osmond, was a great defensive player, and I saw his games regularly. I was so enthusiastic about soccer that I raced through my chores around the house and finished my homework with lightning speed throughout the week, so my parents would allow me to go and play street soccer. On vacations, my friends and I played daily: rain or shine. It was this carefree playing---just for fun, joy and excitement with friends, without coaches, referees or proper equipment---that nurtured my pure love for the game. This was how I contracted the bug for the sport. My enthusiasm led me to want to play for my town team and high school.

When I joined the Iere High School Soccer Team, it was a dream come-true. The school had been without a team for over ten years. The other players and I decided to form a soccer team, and whenever we practiced, we realized how much talent the team possessed. We approached a couple of teachers for help with the administrative steps, such as registering the team and acquiring uniforms and equipment. The team turned out to be number one in the country and is still a legend to this day. People who were not even born at that time know about Iere High School's national champion soccer team of 1973. The team won every game, scored forty-seven goals and only allowed two goals. There hasn't been a team like that since.

When Larry and Charisma spent summers in Trinidad, Larry played a lot of street soccer with Raz's brother Jamal and his friends. Larry said Jamal planted the seed that grew into his passion for soccer. Imagine our joy when we learned that soccer was a popular sport in Massachusetts and enrolled Larry in the town league. These two events coupled with my passion for the sport nurtured Larry's desire to play.

A few years later on a visit to Trinidad, we went to Iere High School, where I proudly showed Larry and Charisma my soccer team's picture and trophies in the principal's office.

Charisma said, "I was very proud to see that picture. Dad talks about that season so much, and it was nice to see him at a time in his life that was so important."

Larry said, "It motivated me to continue the soccer tradition in my generation."

When Larry was about ten years old, he came to us with his goals for soccer. He wanted to play at the town-league level, the Massachusetts-club level, the Marlboro High School Varsity level, the university level, the Olympics and World Cup Soccer level internationally. The Federation of International Football Association (FIFA) World Cup tournaments had a great influence on his desire to play the sport.

One afternoon after commanding the soccer field with his fellow soccer enthusiasts, Larry tossed his gear across his back, and we walked to a nearby wooden, three-tiered bench that emptied of parents and other family members within minutes. Larry climbed to the second tier and placed his gear on the bench beside him. I followed, curious.

"Dad," Larry signed excitedly, "can we have a serious father-to-son talk?"

He was eleven and well accustomed to such talks. At the time, I didn't know this one would last over an hour.

"Sure, son. What's on your mind?" I signed, glad the afternoon wasn't scorching being the stands didn't have an overhead covering.

"I'm like you, Dad. I'm a soccer player through and through. It is in our blood. I can break records just like you, too."

"True. All true. And honestly, you're already better than your old man." I laughed, and then added, "That is how life works. The coming generation is or should be better than the one before."

101

Larry smiled, nodded his head and signed, "You're right. And Dad, I've decided that I 'm not going to focus on my schoolwork from now on. Since I know in my heart that soccer is my passion, I'm going to give soccer 100 percent of my time because my goal is to be a professional soccer player."

For a long while, I said nothing, only looked into his eleven-year-old face, serious and undaunted. I waited for the perfect words and eventually signed, "Larry, you know I support your dream. I want it for you as much as you want it for yourself, but your education is very important, son. Never forget the sacrifices your mother and I made to come here so that you could get the best education."

Larry waited patiently for me to pause before gazing out across the lonesome soccer field outside of a small knot of players practicing drills as their younger siblings chased one another nearby. He made no response.

"Even if you make it to the pro level, there is always the risk of injury, being cut from the team or experiencing a loss of interest in the game. Not only that, your Deafness presents additional challenges. Why limit your options so soon? You have a bright future in academics and soccer. Why not shine in both?"

Larry remained silent, as if he were searching the distant trees along the outskirts of the field for answers.

I put my hand on his shoulder. "Larry, please understand me, son. This is painful for me to say to you, but I wouldn't be a good father if I didn't tell you the truth. Do you understand?"

When he turned to face me, I knew he understood the significance of the conversation clearly. Tears glistened in his eyes. In a silent togetherness, we sat there for a while longer before finally rising to head home. From that day on, Larry planned his life with education as a top priority. He learned to balance his passion for soccer with his education, excelling in both.

Along the way, we continued to support his dreams and guide him to the best of our ability. Still, we recognized the importance of allowing him to take the lead in making decisions about how to manage his soccer career. In the end, he accomplished all of his soccer goals except playing in the World Cup.

As Larry pursued his goals, he experienced opportunities and challenges. His initial challenge occurred when he was deliberately left out of the town's All-Star Team. The previous season, he was one of the top three players on his team. However, the next season when the All-Star Team was chosen, Larry was not selected.

As Larry's parents, we advocated for him to be included on the All-Star Team. After two weeks of negotiating with the town officials, Larry was allowed to play. We had no way of knowing the significance of this opportunity. We only knew that it was our responsibility to help our son fulfill his dreams. Upon reflection, we realized that if he had not been a member of this team, it would have derailed his long-term plans. Each of us learned an important lesson about the power of persistence. We were willing to fight for his dreams. And in so doing, we turned the challenge into an opportunity.

Larry's success on the All-Star Team was a pivotal point in his soccer career. The coach of the team, who was also the coach of Marlboro High School team, invited Larry to play on the junior varsity and varsity teams after only six minutes of play as a substitute on the first day. Also, while Larry was on the All-Star Team, he was recruited by a Massachusetts Division II team. Two of his goals manifested while he was a member of that All-Star Team.

Larry enjoyed playing junior varsity and varsity soccer at Marlboro High School. He improved his soccer skills under a coach who valued his skills and talent. The coach and senior players loved and embraced him because they admired his passion for soccer. When the coach retired, the playing field changed.

Pressure mounted against Larry. A new coach was hired. The athletic director and various parents said Larry should not be on the Marlboro High School team. The politics of the situation took center stage, rather than the talent, ability, and experience of the players.

At the start of the school year, the varsity team scheduled one week of practice. When Larry showed up for practice, the athletic director told him he was not on the team and could not join the practice. The athletic director said the waiver for Larry to play on the Marlboro High School team was not approved for that school year. We lived in Marlboro, and the Marlboro School System sent Larry to the school for the Deaf in another town. In the past, Marlboro High School had applied for and received a waiver for Larry to play soccer. Despite the politics behind the scene, Larry showed up to practice every day, sat on the sidelines and watched the team practice. All he wanted to do was play soccer.

One day a gentleman observing the team practice began a conversation with Larry using paper and pen. He introduced himself as Hank and asked Larry why he was not participating. After Larry explained the situation, Hank suggested that Larry challenge the waiver denial. He also gave Larry his phone number to follow up. Later when we contacted him, Hank and his wife offered wonderful tips on how we might go about the challenge process. When we called the Massachusetts Interscholastic Athletic Association, we were surprised to learn that the waiver was already approved. The following day we requested an audience with the Marlboro Superintendent of Schools, and as a result of that meeting, the athletic director was reprimanded for his poor decision and unprofessional behavior.

Under the influence of the athletic director, the new coach had Larry sit on the bench frequently, sometimes with no playing time. However, whenever the coach allowed him to play, Larry's enthusiasm and excitement inspired the team instantly. Sometimes Larry was asked to play for five minutes with the expectation that he would score a winning goal. Fortunately, Larry was always up to the challenge, persistently doing his best, despite the ill treatment.

Larry's experience with the new soccer coach was very hard on our family. It was a tough two years that threatened to break our spirit. Frequently, we found ourselves in Larry's room after games, encouraging him: "You cannot quit! Your goal is to play high school varsity soccer to reach your next goal of playing soccer at the university level. Hang in there, son. Quitting is not an option." Although it took a while, these challenges taught Larry the invaluable lessons of patience, commitment and perseverance at an early age.

While Larry experienced roadblocks at Marlboro High School, he enjoyed success while affiliated with the Massachusetts Club-Level Soccer teams. Larry was the star on the Division II Club Team. A Division I team recruited him, and he performed so well, he received the opportunity to play in Europe. Though these were meritorious feats, Larry challenged himself to reach further, to do better. The next season he was recruited to the Boston Eagles, an elite Division I club. The players and all the coaches, especially his coach, Brian Ainscough, accepted Larry with open arms, because they judged him on his skills and passion for soccer. Again, Larry's persistence paid off. During his tenure with this club, his skills blossomed. Larry went on to play for the USA Deaf Men Olympic Soccer Team and California State University, Northridge (CSUN) NCAA Division 1 Team.

According to Larry, the most important lesson he learned from his experience at Marlboro High School was the tide can change in any situation. Larry realized that it was important to use his mind as well as his athletic abilities. This realization helped him focus on enrolling at a reputable university for soccer and academics. The Boston Eagles coach encouraged the players to excel in their academics.

Larry said, "The coach asked each player where he was going to college. When he came up to me and asked me that question, I had to start thinking about it. I started my research and eventually found California State University Northridge (CSUN), with a Division I NCAA team and about 25,000 students of which about 300 were Deaf students. Cal State proved the motivation I needed to make sure my grades stayed up in order for me to be accepted."

Larry's passion for life and soccer allowed him to experience the joy and gratification which accompanies pursuing and living his dreams and desires. Larry was able to enjoy his crowning moment of representing the USA and wearing the National USA colors of red, white and blue at the Deaf Olympics in Rome, Italy. Although his path was filled with obstacles, he still followed his passion and achieved success.

REFLECTIONS

1. *We have learned that in the pursuit of your dreams you will be tested.* As you read Larry's soccer stories, you saw that they are transformative for people in the special needs community and beyond. They are filled with goal setting, passion, visualizing, commitment, overcoming obstacles and a belief that all things are possible.

2. *As you pursue your goals, there will be times* when the challenges seem insurmountable. This may be a sign that you are close to the

finish line. You must follow your passion, even if the path is filled with obstacles. Many times, opportunities are disguised as challenges. When you overcome challenges, you open the door to your abundance. Following your passion allows you to keep showing up to break through barriers. Use your passion to create new paths. When you follow your passion with commitment, obstacles move out of your way.

3. *Many settle before achieving their goals.* You should always prepare the path you desire for yourself. We encourage you to work to achieve as many of your goals as possible, hold on to your dreams, and live your life with a sense of passion and urgency. The rewards will astound you.

LESSON 7

CONFIDENCE

"Confidence comes not from always being right but from not fearing to be wrong."

~Peter T. McIntyre~

Larry playing soccer for California State University
Northridge (CSUN) in 1997

ALEX

Raz and I have always been attuned to Larry's interests and strengths. As an active toddler, he awoke each morning with a brilliant smile and an exuberance of energy. As he grew older, we paid attention to the activities that captivated him and retained his attention; we noted those activities that held no appeal for him. It was not unusual for us to find him sitting in front of the television, enthusiastically watching sports for hours. Later, when Larry was in elementary school, he played on the school basketball team, but we quickly learned that he was enthralled with soccer.

Soccer helped Larry build his self-confidence. Over time we witnessed his transformation as his confidence grew. He became a really strong person. Larry's love for soccer influenced several areas of his life. He repeatedly saved his allowance in order to purchase his favorite professional soccer teams' jerseys, which he wore to school with pride. He also took a great interest in his body and his health: he learned about eating right and began incorporating more salads, fruits and plenty of water into his diet. When his peers experimented with cigarettes, Larry didn't get involved because his self-confidence would not allow him to jeopardize his physical and mental health.

Here is my conversation with Brian Ainscough, Larry's favorite soccer coach, from the Boston Eagles, regarding Larry, which contains insights into building self-confidence using your passion.

Alex: Greetings, Brian! Thank you for agreeing to speak with me about your experiences with knowing and coaching my son, Larry Stephen.

Brian: I had the chance to meet Larry through soccer, a game about which he was passionate. I was fortunate to meet him.
Alex: What were your first impressions of him, and how did things develop from there?

Brian: Just a little background—when I met Larry, I was coaching at Providence College as the head soccer coach. We were with this Division 1 club-- the Boston College coach and me--and it was a pretty elite club. Obviously, every year we were having tryouts, and your young son, Larry, came along.

I think we met him first at an indoor session, which sometimes makes it difficult to assess the players' skills, because it was a small little gym floor. My first impression of him was that "This fellow is very, very quick, and he's pretty tenacious." When we took our tryouts outside, we got the chance to see how good he was and what his potential was really like as a soccer player.

114

Alex: He was with you for a couple of years, and you both developed a good relationship as coach and player. Share with us some of the stories or some things you remember about Larry playing for you, for example, some of the games and some of the qualities he brought to the team?

Brian: When I met Larry, the first thing I thought was that you could see the passion he had for soccer, a game I also love. He wore this Argentinean shirt to most of our practice sessions. He had this big, big smile on his face, with the long hair that he wore, which was probably because of Batistuta, the Argentinean center forward, who was his idol at the time.

My stories of Larry are about getting to know him as a player. We gave him his position, and it wasn't based on him being Deaf. We gave him his position based on his ability and the potential that we could drag out of him as a soccer player.
Like I said to you many, many times, "Larry is the only player that listens to me compared to most of my other players, and he is Deaf!"

Alex: We use that line all the time.

Brian: I remember days that he really just wanted to play. I used to have to calm him down an awful lot because he was so feisty and tenacious, a little bit overly aggressive in his tackling, and that's where I had to curb him back.

He was a forward but played a lot like a defender at times because he was aggressive going after the ball. Part of my job in working with him was to calm him down because he might end up getting too many yellow cards or red cards at that time.

Alex: I remember during a specific game you put him in to play defense. After the game, you asked Larry, "How did the game go?" and he said, "Oh, it was okay." You said, "But you had a good game?" His response was: "Yes, but I'm not defense."

Brian: I know, but again, his tendencies were that he was such an aggressive-type player, he could play that. His skills lent to him being a forward, but sometimes his tendency meant that he could play at the back as it went on. Another thing I recall is how the rest of his teammates talked to him. I can't recall a time when we said, "Okay, Larry is Deaf. Larry has this disability."

Before he even got to me, whatever you and your family had done for him, his confidence was always very strong. He was sure of himself. When I talked to him with you as my interpreter, I never really held back or felt like that was getting in the way of his progress.

Alex: He never let that hold him back on the team. Brian, I must say quite candidly that the instructions you gave to the team set the tone from day one. I remember the first day Larry came to the indoor tryouts. I didn't know you, you didn't know me and you'd never met Larry. You told the guys, "Make sure you pass the ball to him when the opportunity arises; treat him as an ordinary player." You set the tone for acceptance, and I must give you credit for that.

Brian: I get credit? When a young man like Larry comes back and calls me his favorite coach, I say maybe he hadn't had that many coaches in his day. I'm very happy that I got the chance to be around Larry. He wasn't just around me for soccer. He was around me for a lot of things. I think I talked to Larry (and this is funny) more times than I talked to most of my hearing players at that time. I remember opening my phone and waiting for the interpreter to come on, and I'd have conversations with Larry, whether they were about games or furthering his academics.

I don't know sign language. But strangely, he always knew what I was thinking. And I knew what he was doing.

Alex: I know both of you respected each other. He saw the passion for the game in you, and that's what he liked.

Brian: To me, there are always things that get us through life. Typically, it's following the things that you're passionate about. I could tell that Larry probably played with a ball since day one and hasn't stopped to this day. With his passion for the game, he got the most out of his game in the sense of what he did every day.

He came to practice with a smile on his face, and he worked harder than everybody. I knew--no matter what he was going to do after leaving me--that he was already successful, no matter what job he decided to undertake. I was hoping it would be some type of coaching job. He went through college and soccer was still a part of his life. Somehow, I always felt he might be teaching the game at some level.

Alex: He did coach at the Learning Center for the Deaf in Framingham. And they won two championships when he was head coach.

Brian: Alex, you were at all the games because you were my assistant coach. You actually did more than just be the interpreter. You were giving me a lot of great support. You were there at the games; your eyes were on the games all the time. What was Larry's best moment that you recall? Any particular one that you have any fond memories of?

Alex: When you guys were in the playoffs, he was having a fun season, but for some reason, he didn't think he was delivering enough. I remember, in Connecticut, he scored this goal and the whole energy changed for Larry and the rest of the team. He was running around---he even did this when he played varsity and the referees allowed him to do this---and you made a comment: "This guy is like Valderamma. He scored one goal, and he's running around the whole field."

Brian: That's right, and that's the reason I asked you because I wanted it to come from you. He puts so much pressure on himself to succeed. We were a high-level club in Massachusetts and New England. He always felt that he wasn't giving enough. We talked about it, and I said, "Hey, relax. You're doing fine!" But he always felt like he could be doing more. He used to get frustrated with that at times.

I saw him grow from someone that came in a little bit tentative in what he was doing, to someone that became very, very confident. I was confident enough at the end of the day to say, "Do you want to come to Providence College, so we can get you into our group?"

He was like, "No." Mr. Independent wanted to go a little bit further away to California. I recall calling the coaches from Cal State, because I had a top player with a disability, like being Deaf, I knew that they would want to be assured that if they took him on, that this kid could get the job done at that level, which is the highest level outside of professional in this country.

I was there letting them know that this young man had the potential to play at that level and make the squad. I know the obstacles that coaches have. Are they willing to go the extra mile to help this person who has a disability?

Alex: Yes, he did very well at Cal State Northridge (CSUN). Brian, we're talking about how you have seen him develop. I've always wanted to ask you something. Have you ever had any experience with a Deaf player or played with somebody who was Deaf in Ireland or in the United States in your soccer career?

Brian: No. Larry was the first one that I can recall. The obstacles he had to face were in the sense of playing a game that's communicated not just through body language, but verbally, especially being European. A lot of times down in South America and in the Caribbean, it's done differently. They don't talk as much as we do, but being European, we're constantly getting our players to talk and communicate.

I was thinking: "How is he going to get over these obstacles?" But Larry had a funny way of making himself heard on the field at all times, and he was probably the loudest of all the players. When he was open, we all knew that he was open.

Alex: Any other stories you remember about him?

Brian: I just think it's fabulous that somebody like Larry comes along, and when I see what he gets out of his life, he puts me and people like me to shame. I see what he does, even now at this stage. But even when I was dealing with him, I was like, "This young man gets an awful lot done! There are no obstacles that remain in front of him."

It was great because he was able to give me tools to teach my other players and even my own children as I became a father and my kids were small. People complain about obstacles being in their way, but here's a young man who wants to play a game that, traditionally, to get to a high level, you need balance. But his balance was tremendous, and he had the speed; so he was able to get the most out of it.

He made me look at myself and think: When I feel sorry that a day isn't going right and I can't get ahead, I think of Larry, who was able to push through countless obstacles. Selfishly, I got an awful lot more from young Larry than he got from me. It was very good for me to know Larry.

"You have to have confidence in your ability, and then be tough enough to follow through."

~Rosalynn Carter~

REFLECTIONS

1. *Most of us admire self-confident people, as* confidence is important in all areas of life. It helps you to be successful, and when you are, people are inspired. Your confidence shows up in your behavior, in the way you speak and in the words you choose. When you are confident, you accept tough challenges and remain persistent. You cope with whatever life brings your way, and you are willing to seize opportunities.

2. *Confidence can be learned. Doing so requires* a shift in mindset. We begin by believing in our ability to achieve our goals and dreams. We use focus and determination to move us forward. Make the commitment to grow your confidence. Start by reflecting on your successes, achievements and strengths. Look for role models and mentors, who are self-confident and learn from their experiences. Work to obtain the knowledge needed to achieve your goals and maintain a positive mindset. Reward yourself when you have success by celebrating with joy.

3. *As you build your self-confidence, reflect on* who and what helped your confidence as you were growing up. Was it your parents, grandparents, teachers, or coaches? It would be wonderful if we could go back in time and

get more of the positive influences and less of the negative. Unfortunately, that is not possible. But we can consciously decide to have a positive impact on our children and other young minds.

4. *Pursue your goals with a burning passion.* As you develop your abilities and skills, you will increase your confidence and achieve your success.

5. *Reflections 5, 6 and 7 will review some* methods of building our children's confidence and independence. Allow them to make decisions. When we allow our children to select their own clothes or hair styles, this sets the stage for bigger decisions. Your objective is to build their confidence in their decision-making ability.

6. *Another way to enhance your child's* confidence is by recognizing and supporting their individual talents and passions. Do they love a specific sport? Are they always singing and dancing around the house? Are they fascinated with food and cooking? Or maybe they are engrossed with building things. Do you know your children's passions? If not, ask them, and explore the possibilities with them. Recognize that their interests may change over time. Go with the flow and support them.

7. *An amazing thing is that your child will listen* to you as well as to his coaches, instructors, and other role models in their areas of interest. These people become allies and help to increase your child's confidence. Your child's high confidence pays off when he becomes a teenager. It helps him cope with peer pressure, school and setting and achieving his goals. A healthy self-confidence will carry him through life.

"You are the only person on earth who can use your ability."

~Zig Ziglar~

Alex, Raz, Larry and Charisma Stephen

LESSON 8

PERSEVERANCE

"Many of life's failures are people who did not realize how close they were to success when they gave up."

~Thomas Edison~

Alex, Raz, Larry and Charisma Stephen

Alex and Raz graduated with top honors at the 1987
Howard University commencement

RAZ

When we left our home and immigrated to the United States, our primary goal was to provide Larry with an educational foundation that would allow him to become independent. In order to reach that goal, we knew we had to excel academically. This would allow us to compete successfully for the best jobs in our chosen fields. We persevered through college with visions of better days for ourselves and our children.

Leaving behind eighty and ninety degree temperatures, we arrived in Washington, D.C., in the middle of winter. Our new home was freezing. In a drug-infested neighborhood, we rented a one-bedroom apartment. The landlord told us the heat was included. We were happy because that was good for our budget, but once we moved in, we were disappointed that the heat for our apartment and the whole building went on only from 6 AM to 6:30 AM daily. This experience was really hard for us. The sheets were ice cold. To stay warm, we slept in the same bed, and more often than not, found it more comfortable to study in bed as well.

We bought our furniture at the Salvation Army. One day Larry was jumping on the sofa, and we heard a sudden crunching sound. Alex and I looked at one another, thinking the jumping had affected the sofa's frame. Slowly, we looked under the cushions, and to our surprise, there was a dead mouse. Another day, we came home to find the kitchen ceiling lying atop the stove. And on another occasion, Alex went to the basement to do the laundry and came upon drug addicts and winos. After that, he began taking the bus to the Laundromat.

Due to the low temperatures in our apartment, Larry developed constant ear infections. Whenever his condition required medical attention, we had to take several buses to the emergency room at Howard University Hospital, because it was the only hospital available on our student health insurance. Once we were signed in at the Registration Desk, we'd spend hours in the Waiting Room, praying to see a doctor, and sometimes this was right before a major exam at school.

One night, Alex took Larry to the emergency room instead of studying for an exam that was scheduled for the following day. He and Larry returned home well after midnight, Alex knowing he had a Business Law exam in a few hours. He considered making a request for a make-up exam but reconsidered. After he took the exam and the grades were announced, the class was informed that only one student received an A. That student was Alex Stephen. He was surprised and relieved. At the end of class, Alex shared the story with his professor, who was amazed that Alex had not asked for a make-up test. We learned to persevere very early in the process and stay prepared, because we never knew if we would have the luxury to prepare for a test the night before.

In my Differential Equations class one Monday, Mr. Donaldson, the chairman of the Math Department, substituted for my regular professor. After class, he and I left the classroom together, heading in the same direction. He asked me to walk with him. I started to introduce myself, and he interrupted me, saying, "I know who you are. You have a 4.0 GPA."

I was taken back that Mr. Donaldson knew who I was. Simultaneously, I was excited that the chairman of the department was aware of my hard work and interested in my story. I told him about Alex and our two children. After a few moments, he asked, "How are you making out financially?"

"Well, Alex has been looking for another part-time job."

"Why don't you bring him to my office tomorrow?" Mr. Donaldson suggested, and I thought I'd explode with elation.

"Yes. We will be there."

When we arrived the next day, Mr. Donaldson said he needed some accounting work done in the Mathematics Department and offered Alex a part-time position. Later, we learned that he created that position for Alex. The income from that part-time job helped us meet our expenses for the next three months. It was a huge blessing!

We persevered through school while working several part-time jobs. I worked in the language lab and tutored mathematics on campus, while Alex worked in Howard University's administration offices, at various parking garages, at a Toyota car dealership washing cars, at a printing factory, as a security guard and at Howard University's convention center as a waiter. And through it all, we maintained superior grades.

Finally, we were living our dreams: our son was attending the best school for the Deaf in the world, our daughter was attending a great Montessori school and we were completing our college degrees. Alex and I were on an unstoppable mission.

Deep into our studies and working, we were surprised to learn that I was graduating Suma Cum Laude with a Bachelor's degree in Mathematics and a minor in Computer Science. Alex graduated Magna Cum Laude with a Bachelor of Business Administration in Accounting and was a member of several business and accounting honorary societies. Just after graduation, Alex got his Certified Public Accountant (CPA) license and took a position with Touche Ross, a prominent accounting firm. In the meantime, I pursued my Masters in Computer Science at Howard University School of Engineering.

Our burning desire and perseverance allowed us to attain our goals. As we persisted, we realized that our prayers were being answered. When Larry graduated from high school, he was the class valedictorian with a 3.5 GPA. He also received the first Gallaudet University Regional Center Award for being a potential leader. Although we had prayed for Larry to be an independent adult when he turned eighteen, his achievements superseded our wildest dreams, and at seventeen, he headed to California State University in Northridge, on the opposite side of the country.

ALEX

About six months before my father-in-law died, he came to the United States for Larry's graduation from California State University Northridge (CSUN). This was his first visit to the Unites States. We had a conversation that I will always remember.

"Alex."

"Yes, sir."

"I want you to know that I am proud of Larry and Charisma. Your children are wonderful. You and Raz are to be praised for the outstanding job you did raising them," my father-in-law said from a sofa in our living room.

"Thank you, sir." Returning his smile, I could see that he was genuinely pleased. Farook was a man who lived his life rooted in gratitude. My mind skirted the years, and suddenly I felt the joy of the prayer meetings he hosted whenever a family member accomplished something laudable, like an outstanding academic achievement or returning home for a visit, etc. "I appreciate that," I confessed.

"And I appreciate you and Raz. You both have accomplished so much on your own, at home and here in the States."

"Yes, sir."

Farook smiled, his face older but still vibrant. "I must admit that I admire you doing what you had to do to assure your family experienced an opportunity many will never have in Trinidad. We are all proud of you."

Again, I thanked him, clasped my palms together, and leaned forward on a chair across from my father-in-law.

"I admire how you and Raz financed your way through college here in the United States, too." He paused, taking me in quietly for a few minutes, and then continued, "Alex, you are a son to me, and you are the best. While I am sharing these things with you, I will admit that I have always admired your compassion."

When he fell silent again, with his hands resting atop his knees, I took a deep breath and admitted, "I have admired you for the exact same reasons, sir."

I did not know that this would be one of our last conversations. It took place in May 2002. Our family was planning to visit Trinidad in December. Larry and Amrit, his lovely fiancé, were planning a January wedding. My father-in-law asked if he could host a wedding reception in Trinidad for relatives who could not travel to Larry's wedding in the United States. We agreed without hesitation.

Love flowed full circle, providing closure. My father-in-law was meant to be the Master of Ceremony (MC) for Larry's reception. The first person he asked to be the MC had to attend another event, the second person developed laryngitis the morning of the reception. Following a brief discussion, my father-in-law and I agreed simultaneously that he should be the MC. In hindsight, I realized that this was his time for closure. He'd host the reception for his first grandchild and close the gap on the reception he never hosted for Raz and me.

Larry and Amrit had a grand reception. Our family from both sides and countless friends were there. My father-in-law was in a good mood. He recognized everyone in his family, starting with his wife and all his children, then all his grandchildren, all the in-laws, one by one, name by name, and said something good about them. Not only that, he stood the cost of the entire gala. It was a wonderful day. Then suddenly, two weeks later, my father-in-law died.

Many people admired my relationship with my father-in-law. I think the foundation of our mutual love and respect was that I respected that Raz was his firstborn, his beloved daughter. My relationship with my father-in-law taught me that I shouldn't fear standing up for my beliefs, that when I persevere and stand up for my beliefs, people will respect me for it. For no one is wrong; we simply have different opinions.

"Perseverance is not a long race; it is many short races one after another."

~Walter Elliott~

REFLECTIONS

1. *Perseverance is an art that we begin to learn* as babies taking our first steps. As we progress, we learn to walk, run, read, and write. Each new skill requires diligence and persistence to succeed. Those early lessons

give us the confidence and experience to face increasingly difficult challenges as we move from childhood to adulthood.

2. *We often find ourselves at a fork in the road.* On one side there is opportunity for growth; on the other is the option to remain the same and pursue the status quo. Most of us have occasions when we are frightened of the unknown. When you are at that proverbial fork in the road and life offers you the opportunity for new experiences, embrace the unknown, and push forward to reach new heights. After all, it is simply an illusion that we know what tomorrow holds. We must push forward with the strength, faith and courage to believe in our dreams.

3. *Opportunities rarely come to us without the* potential for challenges and road blocks. You will likely be tested in your resolve and forced to make complicated decisions. At this point, if your curiosity is stronger than your fear, you will continue to move forward. You pray for a breakthrough. But, ultimately, you step out on faith and leave your fears behind. Do not pray for fewer challenges; pray for more wisdom. Use negative situations to energize and motivate you. Dig deep inside, and create the mindset to move ahead. Accept the hard

times as part of the journey towards better times.

4. *A driving desire to achieve your goals,* combined with faith and perseverance, makes you unstoppable. Believe it, and it is true! We have lived it. We were so motivated that the obstacles we faced did not stop us. Yes, we have faced hardships, but we dealt with them and kept moving forward because we stayed focused on our goals. Sometimes the challenges slowed us down, but we never gave up. Our perseverance not only got us through the hard times, but it was also apparent to others.

5. *You can achieve your goals. Success is a* mindset, and with that mindset, failure is not an option. Your desire to achieve your goals must be so strong that you view setbacks as temporary. Climb over whatever obstacles you encounter. Stay the course, and move towards your dreams.

6. *Sometimes, we struggle to stay motivated.* When you find yourself there, review your goals. Perhaps they need to be redefined so that you have a clearer picture. Ideally, your goals should fill you with joy and energy. Make sure your Why is strong enough to fuel you. This will enable you to stay focused enough to work late at night or early in the

morning. When you are engaged with your Passion and working on your life's purpose, you will be bursting with energy and ideas. You can provide bountiful solutions and services to benefit you and others. Walt Disney said, "If you can dream it, you can do it." Yes, you can create new opportunities for yourself. You can create a new, happy and successful path.

7. *On certain parts of your journey, you may* need encouragement. Seek the advice of relatives, friends, and mentors who believe in you well enough to help you unselfishly. Stay away from negative individuals who may think you are being too ambitious and aiming too high.

8. *You may also wish to join or create a* mastermind group. A mastermind group is a powerful and often effective tool for generating ideas and moving forward with your goals. The group consists of two or more minds with a shared commitment. You work in harmony with others and provide support, solutions and referrals in a non-threatening atmosphere. This group can help you stay motivated and positive. An effective mastermind group allows you to draw ideas and opinions from the collective wisdom of each member. It also creates accountability.

This can be extremely valuable as you are pursuing important goals.

9. *As you strive towards your specific results,* you will start to experience some form of fear: fear of success, fear of failure, or fear of criticism. Sometimes fear is like an anchor; it can weigh you down and drown you, if you are not careful. Fear is one of the most paralyzing emotions we can experience. It can block your progress. When we experience the crippling effects of fear, our mantra is "When fear knocks, answer with faith!" This technique allows us to put fear to rest and tap into our unconscious minds to see solutions. Try it for yourself. It will change your experience. You will no longer be blocked by fear; you will be fueled by faith.

10. *Replace your doubts with faith, hope,* creativity, determination, and persistence. This will ensure your continued progress. If your current goal is a necessary step on your ladder to reach your bigger goal, stand firm on the path to your dreams. Stay the course. When you hit rock bottom, you often find strength that you did not know existed, for it has been said that necessity is the motherhood of invention.

11. *Remember that faith has no limits.* Jeremiah 29:11 says, "For I know the plans I have for you, says the Lord, plans for welfare and not for evil, to give you a future and a hope." When we expect miracles in our lives, we see them made manifest every day. Life itself is a miracle. Train yourself to see everyday miracles and then you will be able to see the extraordinary ones as well.

12. *Keep moving forward, as there is always light* at the end of the tunnel. Do not let others or circumstances take away your dreams or prevent you from achieving your goals. Remember, this too shall pass! Each experience prepares you to overcome bigger challenges. Learn as much as you can from the experiences. Thomas Foxwell Buxton said, "With ordinary talent and extraordinary perseverance, all things are attainable." You must persist to achieve the results you desire. With perseverance, you will win. Perseverance leads to success, for when the world says give up, hope whispers, "Try it one more time."

LESSON 9

GRATITUDE

"Give thanks for a little, and you will find a lot."

~The Hausa of Nigeria~

Alex serving as a banquet waiter on his part-time
job at Howard University

ALEX and RAZ

When we made the commitment to leave everything in Trinidad and immigrate to the United States, we did not have the answers. We had tears in our eyes and courage in our hearts. We had faith, trust, love and gratitude. We thought positively as much as we could. We were grateful for everyday and the opportunities that came our way. By placing ourselves squarely in the flow of life in America, the land of opportunity, we became both an inlet and outlet for the abundance of the Universe to work through us.

"The more you praise and celebrate your life, the more there is in life to celebrate."

~Oprah Winfrey~

We realized how powerful gratitude was the summer before our last semester at Howard University. We were prepared to graduate in December of 1986, and nothing was going to circumvent us from doing that, but life presented us with a challenge that tested our mettle.

Raz and I were sitting at the kitchen table in our apartment, staring at what was left in our bank account.

"Are you sure that's it?" Raz wanted to know, a worried look clouding her usually sunny beauty.

"That's it," I said, tapping my pencil on the tabletop. "I calculated it several times just to be sure, and it still comes up $48.00."

"Honey, I'm grateful for even that, but we just have so much due right now. And there's the children. We've got to keep that in case we need something for them."

"I agree. And we've both got great employment prospects after graduation, but we've got to make it through the summer to even get to graduation day."

The kitchen grew hotter the more we pondered our situation. In the mugginess, Raz ran her hands across her head and lifted the braid on her back, fanning herself. "Let's consider everything pending. Just to be sure of what we're facing. Okay?"

"Okay."

"The rent's due. Our tuition fees are, too. That's roughly $2,000 each. And then there's gas and food and utilities and something for emergencies. Oh, Alex, we just don't have adequate monies to cover it all."

I closed the checkbook. "Right. Our part-time jobs just aren't enough. But we'll think of something.

We've come too far to think of anything but accomplishing our goals."

"You know, the frightening thing is we've tried our best. Really. And we're only six months from graduation," Raz reminded me. "We can't quit and go home now."

"True. We will graduate, and we will go back to celebrate in Trinidad. It just won't be now."

"What are we going to do?"

"I don't know, but what I do know is I've got to make more money somehow so we can graduate. Starting tomorrow, I'll inquire about jobs everywhere."

"I'm scared," Raz whispered.

"I'm scared, too," I admitted. "But everything is going to be alright."

The next day, I got busy persistently asking everybody about job leads and, as Raz likes to say, I didn't stop until I found one. As I searched, I never stopped envisioning our graduation day and my full-time employment in Corporate America. I never stopped seeing Larry and Charisma getting an education and living their dreams.

Finally, thankfully, I spoke with a friend, who was also looking for work. He introduced me to his contact from church. In a cordial, telephone conversation, this gentleman recommended me to serve as a waiter for a catering company at school. I graciously accepted the opportunity, which required I own a tuxedo, and there was only $48.00 in the family account.

Raz and I shared our dilemma with a fellow classmate, Clarence. He was a good friend, always helping us with the kids by dropping them home when I had to be in school.

He said, "Alex, I can help you, but I have no money."

"Well, how will you do that if you have no money?" I inquired.

"I have a credit card. We could put the tuxedo on it, but you would have to pay me back in a month."

"Deal." I was willing to take a chance, no matter what.

RAZ

Alex and Clarence went to the mall on Friday evening, and Alex started the new job that night. The new job paid cash, so Alex worked breakfast, lunch and dinner, the whole weekend. And as promised, he paid Clarence back on Monday at school. Clarence was an angel in our life; he was ever ready and willing to help us.

This job provided all the money we needed to meet our expenses and graduate on time. It was the perfect job for our situation, providing cash and food left over from the functions. The kids and I waited excitedly for Alex to come home. Before us, he would spread an assortment of cheese, chicken wings, chilled shrimp, crackers and an array of fruit.

While the cash and food were stupendous, the trade off, however, was Alex sacrificing studying and taking exams without his usual thorough preparation. His grades slipped, but he had established an excellent foundation early on, thereby maintaining his Magna Cum Laude recognition. In addition, he had already been inducted into the business and accounting honor societies. His interviews with the Big 8 accounting firms, as well as other corporations, were assured. He was not going to fail, not with the finish line so close. Throughout this stressful time, Alex and I remained grateful. After all, we still had a chance, friends, each other, our kids, good grades, our health, and an apartment. The more grateful we were, the more faithful we were that it would all work out.

ALEX

I was grateful for the interviews, especially a major one with Brian Anderson, a partner at the firm Touche Ross. Dressed in a blue business suit, white shirt and red tie, my goatee shaved, I was nervous but ready.

I arrived early and began feeling more at ease while sitting in a brightly decorated reception area. Mr. Anderson didn't keep me waiting. When he appeared before me, his presence filled the room, and he shook my hand and introduced himself, inviting me into his office. The interview began promptly, but after five minutes, he pushed back in his chair and said, "I see you have a 4.0 GPA in your major, and you come highly recommended by the Accounting Department. Tell me how you came to study in the US and how you financed your education."

Nodding, I said, "Both my wife, Raz, and I are in school full time at Howard University. On Saturday, January 8, 1983, we left everything and everyone we knew in Trinidad, almost 4 years ago. With two kids, one Deaf, no extended family, working part time, living in a rough area of Washington, D.C., we learned to survive in a cold, foreign climate. She is Suma Cum Laude in Mathematics and Computer

Science, and as you can see, I am Magna Cum Laude in Accounting. We made it with the grace of God."

Mr. Anderson leaned over the desk with his bulging eyes. "Did your parents or relatives help you financially?"

"No, sir. We saved money before we came to the USA by working full time jobs, and I drove a taxi nights and weekends in Trinidad to save money as well. Then when we arrived in D.C., my wife and I worked part-time jobs. Through it all, we cared for our family and maintained high grades so that we would be qualified to receive tuition scholarships after our freshman year."

Brian Anderson rose, removed his jacket (the room was warm) and invited me to do the same. Thinking it was a test and remembering my business training to exercise the best manners, even though I was sweating, I said, "I'm okay. Thank you."

"Alex, it's okay," Anderson assured me, observing my perspiration. "You have the job! Congratulations. There is nothing you cannot do in life! The second interview is just a formality."

My heart was thumping in my chest. Was this real? Did I actually have the job? In a state of shock, I politely said, "Thank you." Then I allowed my eyes to take in the huge, impressive windows behind Mr. Anderson's desk. The afternoon was clear and blue, the sky sunny. And as natural as breathing, I whispered, "Thank you, Lord."

Everything had come full circle. Gratitude was the key! This was an unimaginable miracle---to have received the prized job seemingly so effortlessly. It had happened in ten minutes! And to think, just three to four months prior, Raz and I were facing the possibility of not graduating.

RAZ

Whenever we think of gratitude, Alex and I think of Charisma, telling her sixth-grade teacher that her parents were her role models. After Charisma shared her role-model story with us, years later, we got another surprise from Larry. On his wedding day, during his speech, he thanked us for everything we sacrificed to ensure his future was bright and limitless.

Larry ended his speech with:

> *"When my parents and I went to Gallaudet University's campus, they saw many independent Deaf people with their own professional careers. The visit impacted my parents,*

and they gave up their lives
in Trinidad to pursue a new
adventure for our family in
the United States of
America."

In that moment, we had many reasons to be proud of our son, as he stood before us, a successful, grown man, taking on a wife. As parents, we are honored when our children thank us for raising them well.

Many years ago, one of Alex's old clients resurfaced and expressed to him that she was depressed because she had lost her business, home, car, and family. She was at her lowest point. Repeatedly, she asked herself, "What did I do to deserve this?"

Alex encouraged her not to take any of it personally. "It is not the end of the world," he assured her.

They discussed the Law of Attraction and the power in practicing an attitude of gratitude to move her forward.

"Alex," the client said, "I wish I could say otherwise, but I have nothing to be grateful for."

Alex smiled and asked, "Did you sleep in a bed last night? Are you using the restroom without assistance? Did you eat breakfast this morning? Didn't you have access to a phone to place this call to me?"

The client remained quiet for a long moment. Then Alex shared the concept of the Gratitude List and its impact on his life.

"Every day, on a single sheet of paper," he said, "draw three columns. In the first column, make a list of ten things for which you are grateful, no matter how big or small. In the second column, make a list of your desires. In the third column, keep track of your manifestations, for doing this will give you a sense of accomplishment and encouragement."

He could see she was attentive, quietly taking in his words.

Two days later, the client called Alex again, but this time she was extremely excited. She shared her belief that for the first time she had a tool that worked.

"When I called you two days ago, I'd contemplated suicide. Your Gratitude List saved my life."

That same client admitted that she had been trying to quit smoking for the past thirty-five years, to no avail. Alex told her that she had to decide that she wanted to quit. In addition, Alex encouraged her to meditate, exercise, pray and to start eating healthy. After six months, she called Alex again. Not only had she quit smoking, but she had also stopped drinking, was eating healthy and working on reconciliation with her husband.

"Many people who order their lives rightly in all other ways are kept in poverty by their lack of gratitude."

~Wallace Wattles~

REFLECTIONS

1. *A feeling of warmth may overcome us when* someone expresses sincere gratitude for something that we have done. We often get that same feeling when we acknowledge someone else. It is even more powerful when you find yourself thankful for the gifts in your life. Gratitude is a high-energy, positive vibration of thought. It is one of the most powerful laws of the Universe. It shifts our vibration and allows us to experience inner joy and happiness. Gratitude, in conjunction with the law of attraction, amplifies the power available to us.

2. *Have you ever found yourself asking, "How* can I rise above this painful experience?" We believe learning to manage our feelings is an important part of life. In order to get into the proper state of mind, it helps to conjure up your memories of hope, love, happiness and

faith. It is important to reminisce on the good in life as often as possible. And this is something that you have to do deliberately.

3. *Reflect on the feelings you have when others* say they love you, or when you say it to others. Think about how you feel after you help someone, or offer kind words to their ears when they are looking for answers. Be grateful for everything in life: loved ones, the ability to communicate, and your financial situation. Regardless of whether you have reached your ultimate goal, learn to be thankful for where you are in this moment. Sometimes we find that what appears to be negative is there for a reason and can be transformed into a positive situation. An attitude of gratitude will evoke pleasant emotions and provide momentum to help you transform your life and create abundance.

4. *Ask and it shall be given. When you ask the* Universe for anything, follow the request with appreciation for what you already have. Also, express gratitude for the fulfillment of your request. Things manifest in our lives when the presence of gratitude is clear. When you are specific, your expression of gratitude is more powerful, and the gratitude statement can be as simple as, "I am grateful for my wife, because she is caring, loving and takes great care of me and our children."

The Law of Attraction is one of the most powerful laws of the universe. Whatever you desire, you can achieve. Whenever you feel abundant, then abundance will find you. You attract what you think about, so the key is to think good-feeling thoughts; once you are in that vibration, you will attract what you desire. You can deliberately choose to feel better.

5. *The foundation of gratitude lies in charity, the* laws of attraction, forgiveness, and listening. Charity is a very powerful gift that we give to ourselves. When we give to others, we are allowing new positive vibrations to enter our lives. We are the first beneficiaries of our acts of charity. Whatever we give to others, we are really giving to ourselves. Many of us learn the importance of charity in our homes. Give your children the opportunity to see you give to others, so they can see the importance for themselves. Many people have the misconception that you have to be wealthy to give. Charity has no quantitative value, whether you give a large sum of money or a few extra items of clothing in your closet. Individuals who give their time are also doing their part to make a difference in someone's life. Identify an organization or a cause that you feel passionate about, and seek ways to help that organization or cause improve the lives of others.

6. *Charity means boundless love and kindness to* anyone and everyone. It is the love of God and man. God said when you give charity, you give Him a beautiful gift, which He will return to you multiplied. Charity includes loving thy neighbor as thyself. As you try to improve your situation, and become dedicated to your Gratitude List, think of those less fortunate than you and count your blessings.

7. *Every individual has his own beliefs when it* comes to giving. Our family believes in giving back to God first, through our tithes. It is our belief that God is the source of our supply. Tithing opens the floodgates that pour down blessings into our lives, and it is there that we recognize our dreams and desires have manifested. Start now, no matter how small. Make the commitment.

8. *Before you go to sleep, practice identifying* the positive aspects of your life, and then deliberately release the thoughts into the day. Make it your intention to release negative emotions, sleep in peace and awake in joy.

Having an attitude of gratitude means eliminating resentment or complaints; the two feelings cannot occupy the same space. Gratitude lifts your spirits and shifts your emotions and consciousness. The key is to appreciate what you have, be grateful, bless it and ask for your heart's desire. Gratitude and expectancy made our dreams a reality. Be grateful for what you have and your desires for more will manifest. We challenge you to become a confident and happy giver. Then observe what happens.

9. *This Universe is so abundant, we need only* create, not compete. We once heard a clergyman say that if all mankind, going back to Adam, made all of their requests known to God, the effect would be like a spoonful in an ocean. There is more abundance to go around than you can imagine. In addition, the Universe works by law, not by chance. There are no coincidences in the people who show up in our lives.

10. *One of the most difficult challenges for some* people is finding the ability to forgive. Forgiveness does not require any money, but it can rob you of valuable time and energy. Forgiveness is free, and it only has value when you give it away. When you allow yourself to forgive someone, it frees up positive vibes in your Universe. Learn to forgive yourself for what appears to be mistakes or imperfections. Holding resentment is like drinking poison and waiting for the other person to die. Remember, the Universe is cause and effect, every thought

that we plant comes back multiplied. In short, it is the boomerang effect.

11. *Listening can be developed.* *It shows* appreciation and respect for people, especially those with whom you spend a significant amount of time. Be grateful to the people who listen to you. Make an effort to reciprocate by deliberately developing your listening skills, for to listen is the foundation of change. Without listening, we cannot transform ourselves. It is listening that keeps us young and flexible. To listen to others is the doorway to the flow of love between us. To listen to oneself is the doorway to the infinite flow of love within and between all things. Listen to your mind and body. What are they telling you? Meditation is one of the best ways to be in-tune with your inner voice. Learning to listen to your inner self takes dedication, time and practice, but the rewards are bountiful.

Alex, Raz, Larry and Charisma Stephen

LESSON 10

LEGACY

"We all leave a legacy; consciously decide to leave a positive one."

~Raz and Alex Stephen~

Alex, Raz, Larry and Charisma Stephen

Larry's family picture in Trinidad in 2012

LARRY

My wife Amrit

My wife Amrit and I met at the National Asian Deaf Congress in Washington, D.C. In March 2000, while I was attending CSUN, three friends invited me to join them in attending the Congress. One evening students from Gallaudet University attended a mixer in the lobby at the hotel where the Congress was held. A Gallaudet gentleman, who looked as if he were from Singapore, got my attention.

"Good evening, Larry Stephen," he began, signing. "It is good to meet you. I know you don't know me, but I want to introduce someone to you."

"Okay," I concurred, considering I enjoy meeting different people and experiencing the blessings they bring to my life.

Then he turned and extended his hand to an unassuming, beautiful young woman, who magically appeared by his side.

"Larry, this is Amrit." And without further preamble, he walked away.

Smiling at one another, Amrit and I stood and chatted for a long time. We had similar interests, we found each other easy to talk to, and we felt familiar with one another even though we were strangers. For the remainder of the gala and throughout the week, we found time to enjoy one another's company. As the Congress was drawing to an end, we eventually exchanged e-mail addresses, instant-messenger screen names, and pictures. I returned to California and Amrit stayed in D.C. Via instant messenger and e-mails, we stayed in touch. The more we communicated, the more we got to know each other, until finally we decided to date long distance.

I was so excited about her, I called my mom.

"Mom, I met the woman I am going to marry," I said, enamored.

"Really. How do you know that?" she wanted to know.

"Because I love the way she thinks!"

"You are definitely your father's son. That is exactly what he said after meeting me." My mom smiled. "When you can, you must call and tell your father and me all about it. I'm certain Charisma already knows." My mom and I shared a laugh, a bit more conversation and eventually, disconnected the line.

Amrit and I didn't see much of each other for a long time, but, fortunately, there were a couple of wonderful opportunities. In the summer of 2000, there were tryouts for the US Men Deaf Olympics Soccer Team in the D.C. area. I flew back east for them, and we met for the second time. The reunion held a twofold excitement for me. It was amazing being with Amrit again, and the tryouts were intense. With twenty-two openings on the team, I was unsure whether I was going to make the cut.

On the day of the evaluations, two coaches evaluated each prospect in a private room. Players shared their soccer experience while the rest of us waited, sweating it out. At the end of the evaluations, I learned that I was among the chosen to be on the team. How incredibly excited I was! And although it would be a year, however, before the actual Olympic event happened, I knew I would be returning to D.C. for team practice sessions, which meant more occasions to see Amrit.

I saw her for the third time in the fall of 2000, when Gallaudet was celebrating its homecoming and the National Deaf Men Soccer Team had a friendly match against the Gallaudet Soccer Team. When I flew to D.C. to play in that game, I was enchanted to see Amrit over the weekend and introduce her to my parents.

Imagine Amrit's amazement when she discovered that my parents could sign! Her parents could finger spell but mostly wrote to communicate with Amrit, although once in a while they used a few signs. So, for her, it was a different experience, and I think she was pleasantly surprised to see how easy it was to communicate with my family. As a result, she liked them instantly. When I travelled to D.C. the next spring for the national soccer team practice, Amrit and I relished another beautiful reunion.

Almost instantly, Amrit was openly embraced by my parents and became a part of my family. In May of 2001, she graduated from Gallaudet, applied to TLC in Framingham and was offered a position. I had another semester at CSUN on the west coast and would graduate in December. Since TLC was near my parents' house, Amrit, my parents, her parents and I discussed the situation and decided that Amrit should accept the teaching assistant position at TLC and live at my parent's house. My parents rented a van, drove down to Maryland and helped Amrit move to Massachusetts while I was in California.

As the summer of 2001 and the Deaf Olympics were approaching, Amrit's parents flew from Singapore to Massachusetts to meet my parents and visit in their home. Our families got along well, and especially so because of their cultural and ethnic similarities. Both families were fun and shared a great sense of humor. Everyone enjoyed joking together. In a special sense, Amrit and I found similarities between us and our families, and this helped our families to become closer quicker.

While Amrit and I were both studying for graduate degrees in Deaf Education at McDaniel College, we decided to get married in January of 2003. Because we had relatives in Singapore, Trinidad and the United States, we wondered if it would be possible to get everybody in the same room at the same time for our wedding. Fortunately, our plans worked out, and many of our relatives in Trinidad were able to share in our happiness.

My family, Amrit and I were planning a visit to Trinidad at Christmas 2002. When my maternal grandfather learned of our plans, he had the brilliant idea to host a wedding reception for us in Trinidad, because many of our Trinidadian relatives could not afford to fly to the Unites States for the wedding.

My daughter Raveena

Amrit and I are blessed with our daughter Raveena, a vibrant, lovely blending of three ethnic cultures. She is an American and, as her immigrant parents, we share our birth country cultures with her. In addition, Raveena is being exposed to both spoken English and visual American Sign Language, so she is a mixture of different ethnic and linguistic cultures. Amrit and I are committed to raising Raveena in the best way possible, considering we want her to be independent, and receive the best education. For example, we purchase educational and musical toys for Raveena and, of course, she naturally loves sports. Amrit represented Singapore in the Pacific Countries Games for the Deaf in track and field and swimming and Gallaudet University in track and field. Amrit's love for sports has led her to receive a bachelor's degree in Physical Education. Therefore, with our eclectic backgrounds guiding us, Amrit and I decided that Raveena would attend the daycare at TLC so she could mingle with the children of other Deaf parents and Deaf children.

Since I have become a father, I am more committed to my family and my responsibilities as a husband and father. As a dad, I want good things to happen for my daughter; therefore, I readily expend the energy it takes and proudly embrace the commitment. Also, I believe that good things will not happen without the work and guidance of a father. Amrit and I are teaching Raveena to be independent, so we start by teaching her small skills that will carry her through life. She is three and already knows how to tie her shoes. She knows how to get into her car seat and buckle the seat belt. She is exceptionally bright and has many accomplishments, which I won't list, but I will freely admit that I am a proud father.

We are frequently asked about our experiences and challenges as Deaf parents of a hearing child. Like all parents, we want the best for our daughter. Many things are the same whether you are a Deaf or hearing parent, but there are some things that are different. For example, we communicate in a visual way, and we sometimes use special equipment to communicate. It is part of our life; therefore, we do not see it as challenging.

First of all, we are fortunate to live here in the United States, where we enjoy freedom and respect as Deaf adults and parents. In some countries, Deaf parents of hearing children do not have the same level of freedom and respect. Second, there are many Deaf people with hearing children; we can draw on this resource as a form of support, advice and education in our wonderful network in this brotherhood of Deafness. Living in an age where we have access to international online communities, we are especially lucky.

Amrit and I want Raveena to be confident. One of the biggest challenges for kids of Deaf adults is that they are in two worlds. They are born into a Deaf world, but they live in the mainstream, hearing world. Amrit and I are very active in our local Kids of Deaf Adults (KODA) organization. The main goal of the organization is to teach the kids to be proud of their heritage as bilingual and bicultural children raised in families where they probably learned to sign before they learned to speak English. We want to help our children form a positive sense of their identity. We recognize that without this support many of these kids are more likely to develop identity problems. The organization helps to build their confidence by affording them access to peers who have Deaf parents.

Our home

When Raveena was one, we purchased our home and made modifications to accommodate our needs. It is important for us to have a good line of vision of what is happening in our yard and on the street. We removed trees around the house because we wanted to make it brighter and easier to see the entire yard. For example, there was a large tree next to the garage that blocked the view, obstructing our view around the corner onto the driveway; we trimmed its branches to maybe ten feet. The tree is still alive, but we now have a better line of vision from the garage to the driveway. We also had a contractor remove the kitchen, the dining room and the living-room walls to "open" the living area. Doing so is much better for visual communication.

We installed strobe lights in various places throughout the house. These lights allow us to keep track of what is going on in the house. For instance, when Raveena is in her bedroom and we are in the living room, if she cries or makes a noise in her room, that noise will switch the light off. This lets Amrit and I know to pay attention. We have designed the system to blink at different frequencies in response to various sounds such as noise from Raveena's room, a ringing doorbell, the opening of a window or the ringing of the video phone. We have CO_2/smoke detectors installed throughout the house, and these detectors have strobe lights as well.

Family life

Before 2000, I did not have a clear vision of my family life. Eleven years later, I have a home, a wife and a daughter who is already three years old. Raveena has been accepted to a private Montessori school. I was just promoted to a full-time position at Northern Essex Community College (NECC). Never could I have envisioned all of these blessings a few short years before! Today our family future looks brighter than ever. Perhaps Amrit and I will have more children. We feel assured our daughter will have many educational accomplishments. The same as our parents encouraged us, we will encourage Raveena to go to college, discover her passion and use it to identify something that she loves to do in terms of her professional life.

Parental Responsibilities

I believe the responsibilities of parents include the commitment of time and energy to their children to be able to nurture their dreams, to give their children access to both academic and cultural institutions, and to show them the real world and that there are consequences for certain actions in the world. Do not shield them from those consequences. Make sure that your kids have a good educational foundation. Take them on field trips and connect their academic learning to the world they live in. Make sure that you do everything you can and spend as much time as possible to nourish your children, not just with food, but well selected cultural, educational and spiritual experiences for their minds and souls.

To show me what college looked like, to give me a sense of the academic environment so that I would be familiar with it early on, I remember my parents taking me to visit the Howard University campus when I was a kid. This allowed me to have a mental schema of college life.

I also saw my parents get their degrees and had relatives from Trinidad visit for their graduation. I saw this as something I could accomplish in the future and, as a result, I began imagining myself graduating and having relatives attend my graduation.

American Sign Language (ASL)

American Sign Language (ASL) was the key that unlocked the door to my mind; it helped me gain access into the world of thought, which definitely afforded me a better life. ASL is a language of the eyes; you take in information visually. I learned ASL when I was four, after my family and I moved to the United States. Before that I did not have a foundation language. I thought in "pictures" and was unable to express myself. ASL allowed me to express myself and to understand concrete information as well as abstract ideas.

Had I not learned ASL and been exposed to other signers, my ability to read and write English or any other language would not have been effective and my world would have remained closed in a fundamental way. Once I had the foundation of ASL, I was able to learn English, Mathematics, Chemistry and other subjects. ASL opened the door to my future life of learning.

Birth to three years is a critical language development period for children. Thus, a child who is born Deaf needs to be exposed to and taught sign language. Using visual language in their infancy and when they are toddlers will open doors to the world for them and give them the ability to learn language and develop communication skills similar to other children. I believe that for Deaf children particularly it is important that they learn ASL as a foundation language. Then they can become bilingual, because, in the end, it is important for Deaf people to be bilingual in English or their native country language and ASL.

Deaf people around the world face many limits in education and opportunities, and the reach of ASL has only gone so far. My hope is that our book will not only help families, but it will also help people understand that ASL is a positive means to communicate with their Deaf children. The power of a book is not just in the reading by one person, but it's the reading by one person who then tells a friend who passes it along to another friend, et cetera. It

175

has a multiplicative effect in this way. We hope to inspire people with our can-do story to change their attitudes, their environment and make changes to achieve their goals. We have overcome every barrier we faced, and we believe you can do the same.

Being Deaf in a hearing world

Many people are probably wondering how it feels to be a Deaf person in a hearing world. If I am in an environment where I am the only Deaf person amongst hearing people, I think the one thing that occurs to me is that we are all human. We all share just about every sense. We can see the environment, we can smell it, we can touch it, and we can feel the humidity in the air. Still, if those people do not use a visual language like ASL, and I do not speak the spoken language they speak, then in that experience we are unable to communicate.

Even though we may be occupying one space, we are unable to communicate. Therefore, I find it effective to take the lead when interacting with the hearing world. I let people know what works best for me. I tell them that I am Deaf by gesturing briefly and then suggesting that we go to a piece of paper so we can communicate better. I believe that it is always incumbent on me as the person who is Deaf to ask for the accommodations that I need. So, I recommend that Deaf people or people losing their hearing be assertive in that way also.

In new situations or situations where I know that communication can be potentially bumpy, I draw upon my experience and knowledge of the environment and offer adjustments to reduce communication difficulties. But, at times, it can be difficult to do so. For example, if I am going into a medical environment for an appointment with a doctor who is not my regular doctor, I do feel a certain level of anxiety because the interaction will be outside of my comfort zone or familiarity. However, if I am going into a situation that is highly predictable and I already have a schematic understanding of it, and I have done it a hundred times before, communication difficulties are minimal.

I must admit that at times it can get frustrating being Deaf in a hearing world. Here is a perfect example: when I go to a fast food restaurant like McDonald's, I get in line to order. The first few people get their order and when it is my turn, often there are people behind me. Sometimes as I am writing out my order, the cashier will ignore me and start serving the person behind me. It can be frustrating to wait in line like everyone else and be ignored when your time comes to order.

In cases like this, I ask the cashier to get the manager. When the person arrives, I explain to him in writing what has happened. In most cases, the manager reprimands the cashier. Even though this example is a small one, it does have a larger lesson. I think a lot of Deaf people are poorly served or discriminated against in small, petty, undignified ways. Many Deaf people just accept these things as part of life. By refusing to accept it and calling the manager, I see myself as an advocate for the next Deaf person that steps into that McDonald's.

Here is another example: NECC has four campuses. I work on the main campus, which has an Interpreter Training Program, and there are Deaf people at that campus. One day, I was teaching an ASL class and one of the students told me that he heard a fire alarm in the hall. I realized only then that the school did not have visual (strobe lights) fire alarms. After the fire drill, I spoke to the fire marshal and the fire inspector. I indicated that I was Deaf and explained that there were other Deaf people in the building. I pointed out that lights should be added so that there is a visual as well as an audio fire alarm for safety. The campus has an American with Disabilities Act (ADA) office, to which I reported the incident. They agreed to work on adding the visual fire alarms.

My positive experiences in the mainstream world outweigh the frustrations. At NECC, I am in a small Deaf Studies program amongst a large number of non-signing people. Of all the community colleges at which I have taught, NECC does offer a Deaf-friendly environment in many ways. This allows me to socialize at work. When I arrive at the Deaf studies lab in the morning, there is a hearing, signing woman who works there, so we sit and talk for a few minutes as you would in any work environment.

I teach my classes and during the day I have the opportunity to chat with peers who are fluent in sign language. Since I have benefited from guidance and mentoring from some of my peers, the environment has been enriching and positive. The Interpreter Training Program at NECC is the longest running program in Massachusetts, running for about thirty years. I enjoy having the opportunity to be a part of the program, especially since things are changing there, and I can be a significant part of that change. I like to teach. I like the environment. I earn respect from my students because they want to learn sign language.

Another positive experience is my church life. Growing up, I had full access to what was going on in the church. We moved to Massachusetts when I was ten years old, and Charisma was seven. We began attending services at the Presbyterian Church in Sudbury. The church did not have an interpreter. After recognizing there was a need in their congregation for an interpreter, Pastor George Saylor and the church school superintendent, Doris Soule, hired an interpreter for me.

Pastor George even visited my school and spoke to my teachers. Doris reached out to one of the teachers at my school and invited her to come to the church and teach ASL classes, which were offered at no charge to the church members. The individuals who took advantage of the class were always excited to communicate with me. Doris would practice her signing in preparation to talk to me, as well as her husband Don, thereby allowing us to discuss our mutual passion, soccer. One Christmas our entire family participated in an advent service. Pastor George made sure I read my own passage. Instead of just selecting Charisma to read, I was included, too.

I felt included with my family in church. I loved to listen to Pastor George, who used humor quite a bit to illustrate his points. Going to church was quality family time, and the quiet, contemplative environment of church encouraged me to think about who I am and what kind of goals and plans I have and could have. I received a good grounding in values from having full access to the church. Amrit and I use these values in our family life. Now Raveena loves church, especially the music.

My goals

I have completed my formal education through elementary, secondary, college and graduate school. Now I am teaching. I do not see this as the end. I see my future in sports, education and family, like a mango tree. I see that the mango tree is growing tall, although it does not have deep roots. Yet I see my goal is to deepen the roots, to strengthen the branches and to produce as many mangoes as possible. Same as that mango tree, I have so much more to accomplish in my life.

One of my passions is to plan and start communities around the world. I am motivated and drawn towards developing camaraderie among Deaf people by creating events, communities or different opportunities for us to come together whether for sports, for the celebration of religious holidays or for cultural activities. My motivation is that I feel good about my community when I do this type of work, and I personally want to meet more people. Generally, Deaf people do not live close enough to each other to have regular opportunities to socialize; therefore, I feel compelled to create opportunities for Deaf people to come together. Amrit and I have worked at creating these opportunities at various locations to give access to as many people as possible.

When Amrit and I finished graduate school and returned to the Boston area, we organized events for the Deaf community to get together to commune and learn about each other's religion, culture and country. Amrit and I, together with friends, organized various celebrations in the New England area for a number of years. Then our efforts evolved into the International Deaf Club of Massachusetts. Today, the organization continues to grow to include many different Deaf ethnic communities.

To use my experience and love for sports to build communities is another personal goal for me. Soccer is not just a sport; it is also an experiment in teamwork. In the past, Deaf people in many Caribbean islands were not able to compete in sports events because of limited opportunities for Deaf athletes. I am able to network with Deaf leaders in various Caribbean islands, using tools such as Internet chat and Skype, to increase these opportunities. For example, in the Bahamas I was able to give advice and encouragement to the Deaf leaders to start a Deaf sports club, with the goal to have their teams participate in the Deaf Olympics. Based on our conversations, the Deaf leaders have set up a Deaf sports club which is active in the World Federation of the Deaf and the Deaf Olympics organizations. The opportunities for Deaf athletes in the Bahamas are now growing exponentially.

I am involved with similar networking to build opportunities for Deaf athletes in Jamaica. The Pan American Games for the Deaf was held in Brazil in November 2011. That was the first time Deaf Jamaicans competed at those games. Empowerment has come in different ways to Deaf people who live in developing countries. I am proud to have come together with other members of the World Congress for the Deaf to encourage and support Deaf athletes to create sports and educational opportunities for Deaf people.

Currently, I am having similar discussions with the Deaf leaders in Trinidad, but they seem to focus more on religious access for Deaf people. There are Christian, Catholic and Jehovah's Witness groups. Setting up a Deaf sports club is a lower priority. When I visit Trinidad, I speak to students, teachers, and parent organizations about my life experience and the opportunities available in the United States. One of my goals is to create communities, online and in person, for Trinidadian Deaf youths to see Trinidadian Deaf adults leading successful lives and to enlist these adults to help the Deaf youths. This effort is similar to the online community, West Indian Association for the Deaf (WIAD), an organization I started while in college. The idea here is to get more in-depth services. For example, to have Deaf adults mentor Deaf youth. Once we have a working model for Trinidad, we can then expand to the Caribbean and other areas of the world.

My other goals include doing as much as possible so that Deaf children have early access to sign languages worldwide and for kids to have a twenty-five-year plan, so to speak, for people to ask themselves, "Do I have access to the appropriate levels of education that I would like to have? Can I find schools that work for me? Are colleges open to me and accessible to me as a Deaf person?" If you do not have these things in your environment, move to a space where you have access to these things.

I have learned that to achieve your goals, you need to surround yourself with the right people. Make sure you understand who you are and what you bring to the game. Your plan may not always be 100% on par, so be prepared to adjust your plan if necessary. If you feel you are stuck in a rut, you need to find new people. You need to find others who share your vision and can help you see different avenues. Collectively, we can overcome our challenges by staying connected to others and creating positive relationships. There are many things that are challenging for us as individuals, but together we can accomplish them. I appreciate the value of teamwork. A strong team can bring out the best in everyone.

REFLECTIONS

1. *I want people to remember my persistence* and that I never gave up on my goals and dreams. You must do the same. Be passionate about something dear to your heart. Be persistent in bringing it to the light, and never give up on yourself, your goals and your dreams.

2. *Plant communities in your life and in the* world. I want to leave people with examples of creating, planting and finding a community. Your sense of community might not be to help illuminate life for Deaf people, but only you

can search your heart to know what it is about which you care. Whatever it is, plant a positive, loving seed for it to grow, flourish and be your legacy in the world.

3. *Finally, I recognize that I will be judged by the* accomplishments of my descendants. So will you. Whatever Raveena and our other unborn children do in the world, it will reflect positively on her, Amrit and me, and the love and support we provided as her loving, caring parents.

CONCLUSION

"Life is not about waiting for the storm to pass; it is about dancing in the rain."

~Unknown~

Entire Stephen Family in 2011

ALEX

It is our sincere hope that as you read our story, you have developed the insight and courage to know that any challenge you may face is not really an obstacle to your success. In fact, we believe that challenges are often disguised vehicles for your blessings. For us, the miracles we received were *unimaginable*. You have the opportunity to *imagine* your miracles and turn any obstacle you face into an opportunity to live the life you desire. When you operate from that place, we believe that you will receive rewards beyond your wildest dreams.

When Mrs. Arneaud told Raz and me, as young parents, that having a Deaf child could be the best thing that ever happened to us, she gave us the courage to move forward. We did not understand the wisdom of her words then, but in time we came to know their profound and prophetic quality. We hope that when you read the final page of our book, you will fully understand that any challenge you may face has the potential to be the best thing that ever happened to you. We hope that this will allow you to wipe away your tears and fill your heart with courage.

We believe that when you put faith first and love second, you can accomplish things beyond your mind's ability to conceive. You enter into a realm of grace, greatness and abundant blessings.

We encourage you to use love to strengthen the foundation of your life and the lives of your family members. Use love as the fuel to commit to your goals, to persist in accomplishing them, to experience fulfillment and happiness and to achieve your full potential.

When you implement the wisdom and lessons from our journey, your children and those around will learn from you. *Automatically,* you will leave a legacy for generations to come. Within you is a treasure trove of riches and blessings. However, you must develop the capacity to tap into the Universal wisdom and enjoy it.

"Everything in the universe is within you. Ask all from yourself."

~Rumi~

Alex, Raz, Larry and Charisma Stephen

BONUS

LARRY STEPHEN

"I don't regret the things I've done; I regret the things I didn't do when I had the chance."

~Unknown~

Helping Deaf Youths:

If you, Beloved Reader, are seeking an opportunity to help Deaf youths, please support people and organizations working to help Deaf youths improve the quality of their lives through education and networking. Deaf youths need to see Deaf adults leading successful lives and functioning as up-standing members of their communities.

I encourage Deaf youths and adults to pursue leadership activities in their community. For example, when I taught in the adult-education program at DEAF, Inc., I organized and supervised extracurricular activities with my students and my colleagues. We started the International Deaf Club of Massachusetts and sponsored various social events on weekends at Deaf, Inc. When the executive director of DEAF, Inc. witnessed our successful accomplishments, she invited me to join their board of directors. We had a conversation, and I agreed to serve an 18-month term on the board. Likewise, you can start by volunteering for small tasks and positions and then expanding your leadership roles.

Extracurricular activities:

I encourage Deaf youths to participate in extracurricular activities at school and at other venues; they will learn many skills that can be used in all areas of their lives. The friends I made through soccer and the academic world have been positive influences in my life, and as a result, I have been a positive influence on others.

Advice to all families, not only those with Deaf Children:

Be critical when making decisions that involve your child's education. Look for the right environment in which the school offers the right curricula for your child's needs and interests. Your child should have the ability to cultivate his own personality in a non-restrictive setting. For example, your child should be encouraged to make his or her own decisions, whenever possible. Make sure your child socializes with positive people. It is important that he is surrounded by people who will support his advancement, not put him in a position to be held back.

Help transform lives from Challenge to Victory:

Never give up hope. Stay focused. During trying times, seek ways to persevere through challenges and frustrations. Use your resources. Remember that others are always available for help, support and consultation. The ability to ask for help is humbling and powerful. Use it as a tool towards the resolution of your challenges. Understand your

history.   Read books about Deaf history.   Google
websites where Deaf people post video blogs to
build a bridge of communication with other Deaf
people. On YouTube, Deaf people from all over the
world tell their stories. Explore Deaf media outlets
like Deaf Nation, which offers an online newspaper
with tips about how to break through some of the
social barriers that Deaf people face daily.

Experiencing Hearing Loss:

If you are experiencing hearing loss, contact The
Hearing Loss Association of America (HLA) and the
Association of Late Deaf in Adults (ALDA).   Both
have chapters in Massachusetts and throughout the
nation.

You must find other people who share your issues or
challenges.   Frequently, some of these people
already have ways of dealing with your challenges,
so don't reinvent the wheel. Form partnerships with
people who share your needs. Invite them to be
your mentors to help you lead a more independent
life and gain the skills you may need for this new
dimension in your life.

I have been asked by adults who have lost or are
losing their hearing, what they can do to keep their
confidence intact.   Sometimes my communication
wavers when I encounter environments where there

might be shaky communication. However, I try to be prepared as much as possible. For example, I recently went to the doctor because of an illness. I knew there would be no interpreter, so I wrote the following information on a piece of paper: when it started, what it looked like, the over-the-counter medication I used and how it felt. When the nurse called me in to see the doctor, I showed him that I use American Sign Language and handed him my notes. The nurse took a look at the paper, and her face was impressed. It was obvious that she understood that I was prepared to be at this appointment. Also, I think she admired my initiative. In short, our shared and overlapping communication worked great.

Be prepared for any situation, and don't fear taking control of the situation. If you don't, the situation will control you, and that's how you lose confidence. The take-charge approach to life is advisable for hearing and Deaf people alike.

Tips and Advice to the Hearing World:

Hearing people can become advocates of Deaf people by listening to what Deaf people say about organizing for social change. If you are in places where Deaf people's access to schools is limited, lobby at the political level to pass laws recognizing Deaf children's rights to schools and visual language, because that is the key to future education for Deaf people. For Deaf people to access their educational rights and make important changes, they need assistance from hearing people to tear down barriers and open doors.

Corporations and Industries:

Service industries should offer diversity training programs that support their employees in recognizing that there are Deaf customers in the world and Deaf customers go to restaurants and stores, get their cars serviced, and do everything that hearing people do. These diversity programs should be taught with training manuals for employees to refer to when they experience challenges with Deaf customers/clients. In actual physical training sessions, employees should be reminded that the business will serve hearing as well as Deaf customers.

In addition, in the diversity-training world, places like the Red Cross, which offers CPR and First Aid Training to the general public, should be mindful to hire and train people who may use sign language or who do not speak English. Trainings should also include interpreters and visual modes of communication training materials with captions, etc., when volunteers or employees are being trained. To be mindful of these training procedures should not be deemed irritations, for the mission of the Red Cross is to assist all people, not just hearing people, who might require help in an emergency.

ABOUT THE AUTHORS

ALEX STEPHEN

Alex is an author, speaker and transformation/lifestyle coach. Passionate about transforming lives around the globe by helping people identify and live their life's purpose, he uses his own life as an example of how to live your purpose and automatically create a legacy for your loved ones. A Howard University honor graduate and a Certified Public Accountant (CPA), Alex built a distinguished, 20-year career in business finance where he held titles such as Corporate Loan Officer and Vice President/Director.

RAZ STEPHEN

Raz is an author, speaker and transformation/lifestyle coach. She joins her husband in touching lives and changing destinies of those who hear and read the awe-inspiring story of their life journey. The dynamic mother, grandmother and business woman holds a managerial position in a major software company. Raz is a Howard University honor graduate with a Bachelor's in Math and Computer Science and a Master's in Computer Science.

LARRY STEPHEN

Larry is an author and a graduate of California State University, Northridge. He holds a Bachelor of Arts in Geography and a Master's in Deaf Education from McDaniel College in Maryland. A renowned athlete, he was a Division I and USA Deaf Olympic soccer player. Additionally, he is a founder and leader in various Deaf organizations, as well as an Associate Professor in American Sign Language at a college in MA.

CHARISMA STEPHEN

Charisma is an author and an honor graduate of Northeastern University, Boston. She holds a Bachelor's in Music Industry and Business. A project coordinator for the state of MA, Charisma is fluent in American Sign Language. She is living her dreams and following her passion in the music industry. And yes, she lives up to her name. Charisma.

LINKS AND CONTACTS

The Stephen Family can be reached via the following links and contacts:

www.LifeTransformingTreasures.com
www.LTT7.com/guide
www.LTT7.com
www.NextLevelRiches.com
info@alexstephen.com
www.alexstephen.com

Mail to:

Life Transforming Treasures Corporation
P.O. Box 157
Marlboro, MA 01752
USA

Alex, Raz, Larry and Charisma Stephen